D1622664

SIMPLE PRINCIPLES™
TO THINK BIG AND
ACHIEVE SUCCESS

Alex A. Lluch
Author of Over 3 Million Books Sold!*

Dr. Helen Eckmann
Doctor of Education and Leadership Science

WS Publishing Group
San Diego, California

SIMPLE PRINCIPLES™
TO THINK BIG AND ACHIEVE SUCCESS

By Alex A. Lluch and Dr. Helen Eckmann

Published by WS Publishing Group
San Diego, California 92119
Copyright © 2008 by WS Publishing Group

Designed by WS Publishing Group:
David Defenbaugh

For Inquiries:
Logon to www.WSPublishingGroup.com
E-mail info@WSPublishingGroup.com

ISBN 13: 978-1-934386-07-1

Printed in China

TABLE OF CONTENTS

Introduction

Everyone in the world wishes to be a success. And yet, many people struggle to label themselves as such. Success isn't a "thing" we bring into our home that stays with us forever. There's no guidebook or set of rules that tells us when we have surpassed the mark. So what does it really mean to be successful? Amazingly, that definition is different for everyone. To some, success is having a pile of money and a big house. To others, success is finding a loving partner and creating a family. Even more interesting are the people who have one or the other and still feel unsuccessful. They feel this way because success truly is unique for each of us. Perhaps journalist Christopher Morley defined success best when he wrote, "There is only one success — to be able to spend your life in your own way." Indeed, whatever you define as successful is what you should aspire to have and become. When you accomplish this you will succeed in anything you want.

What is this book about?

This book is not about how to get rich fast. Even though wealth and success have long been associated with each other, the definition of success is not limited to money. Albert Einstein once said, "Try not to become a man of success, but rather try to become a man of value." This book is about becoming the type of person who fulfills needs, gains skills, cultivates meaningful relationships, and achieves goals. In other words, it is about becoming a person of increased value.

This book will help you to be successful in all areas of life: at work, in school, at home, in social circles, with family, on the job market, and in business. It touches on topics, skills, and values that are shared by successful people everywhere. It will help you improve your communication skills, which are considered to be the gateway to success. It will help you get organized and show you the importance of keeping yourself educated. In reading this book, you will learn how to increase your productivity, develop people skills, and be prepared for both emergencies and everyday realities. You will be encouraged to keep an open mind and learn tools for building your self-confidence.

It will impress upon you the importance of mastering public speaking, the number one fear of Americans. This book advises you on how to go about taking risks, how to become an expert negotiator, and how to create a network of people that can help you succeed in personal, professional, financial, and social endeavors. Finally, you will learn how to set and achieve goals, take initiative to make things happen, develop an attitude for success, and absorb tricks for learning the balancing act that all successful people have mastered.

Throughout this book you will notice one main theme common to successful people: treating people well. Indeed, it is impossible to be successful without treating people with courtesy. You will learn why it is important to treat your friends, family, coworkers, and others with respect. You will also learn why it is important to engage them on personal and professional levels, whether that means to hold their hand, hear them laugh, or clink glasses to celebrate their accomplishments. Successful people become so by cultivating meaningful, collaborative relationships with others — this book will teach you how to do that.

This book will also impress upon you the importance of

developing highly effective habits. Indeed, successful people have integrated certain critical habits into their lives, such as being organized, showing up on time, responding to criticism and feedback, being honest, doing what they say they will do, and taking initiative. Mastering the skills discussed in this book is possibly the single greatest step you can take to become a more successful person.

Lastly, this is a book about learning to capitalize on your strengths. The principles in this book will help you identify the skills you have and put them to use. You will learn to take action, challenge yourself, and exceed your own expectations.

Who should read this book?

Simple Principles™ to Think Big and Achieve Success is for those who want to be happy, healthy, confident, and fulfilled. In other words, it is a book for *everybody*. The information in this book can be applied to high school students who want a head start on leading effective lives; college graduates just starting out in their careers; professionals looking to advance; people looking to do more than just survive; and individuals of all ages looking for profound personal, social, professional, and financial growth.

This book is for people who want to:

- Achieve their desired outcomes more often
- Motivate themselves to do better
- Feel in control of their life path
- Reduce the amount of stress in their lives
- Reduce the amount of conflict in their lives
- Increase confidence in their abilities
- Improve their relationships with people
- Balance the priorities of work and life
- Communicate effectively
- Accomplish more in their day
- Develop a positive outlook on life
- Finish what they started to "close the deal"
- Successfully negotiate what they are worth
- Create a network of talented, useful people
- Set and achieve goals
- Learn organization and preparedness skills
- Inspire others to succeed

Even if you feel like your life has led you to a happy, successful place, you'll find that the 200 simple principles contained in this book will be solid reinforcement for the strategies you already practice. These principles are filled with great tips, suggestions, pieces of advice, and wisdom. They may even shed light on techniques you didn't even know you already use. This easy-to-read, inspirational book is sure to make a difference for people wanting to achieve their goals and make a positive impact in their lives and on others.

Why should you read this book?

Picking up this book indicates you already have a desire to do better in life — that's a great start. What many of us lack, however, is the discipline and commitment to follow through on the things we tell ourselves we should do. Here are some questions to ask yourself if you are wondering whether this book is right for you:

- Are you tired of being passed over for promotions and raises?
- Have you had trouble finding a job?

- Are your ideas taken seriously by others?
- Do you have trouble finishing what you start?
- Do you have trouble comfortably talking to people?
- Do you wish you had a more well-balanced life?
- Do you tend to fall victim to negative attitudes?
- Do you suffer from low self-esteem?
- Is it difficult for you to speak in public?
- Do you want to be more of a risk-taker?
- Do you want to develop networking skills?
- Do you avoid negotiating because it is difficult for you?
- Are you tired of being disorganized and unprepared?

These are just a few of the benefits that you will gain by reading this book. The principles contained in this book are researched and supported with inspirational quotes and statistical information from credible sources. Its size makes it easy to keep with you for quick reference whenever you are facing a situation that needs to be improved. This book can help empower you to make potentially life-changing choices about your future and the way you enjoy it. Finally, you should read this book often so the ideas stay fresh in your mind.

SUCCESS IN
THE MODERN WORLD

Success does not come easily to most of us. Indeed, most people struggle their whole lives to be successful. Many people do things out of desperation, which is surely the wrong path to success. Indeed, examples of how not to be successful are all around us. In their struggle for success, professional athletes increasingly abuse steroids and other performance-enhancing drugs. Politicians are continuously investigated for illegal behavior, such as sex scandals or accepting illegal donations. Increasing numbers of CEOs are being charged with corporate fraud. All of these nefarious activities are undertaken to achieve success. What is even more surprising to realize is that these are all people who have generally "made it" and yet they want more.

Achieving success in our lives is not supposed to be so difficult; after all, we live in the United States of America. We have the American Dream to pursue, which includes getting a job, finding someone we love, buying the house we want, and watching the children play out back with the dog. Most of us grow up assuming that we will attain the same level of success our parents did. But as many have come to realize, achieving success is much more difficult than it used to be.

Why has it become so difficult to be successful?

There is no one reason why achieving success should be so difficult, although it certainly is. Evidence of unsuccessfulness is all around us. In 2007, we saw the highest percentage of foreclosures on home loans in more than 50 years. Gainful employment has steadily become more competitive as globalization has led to increased outsourcing. The industries that are creating more positions — for the most part, in the service sector — pay on average 20 percent less than industries losing the most jobs. These pressures have taken a toll on personal and family lives as well. Since 1960, the number of children living in single-parent homes has tripled from 9 percent to almost 30 percent. And in any given year, at least 18.8 million American adults suffer from some form of depression.

These statistics reveal the gloomy nature of today's world, but that is all the more reason why reading *Simple Principles™ to Think Big and Achieve Success* is one of the best decisions you can make. It will help you, for example, realize why educating yourself is critically important to achieving success. Indeed, it used to be that a high school diploma was enough to enter the workforce. A college degree — from any institution — was just another feather in the cap. These days, however, it is pretty well understood that full-time, salaried jobs require a college degree. Furthermore, the school from which that degree comes from matters even more, since *U.S. News & World Report* began ranking colleges in the early '90s. With college application numbers up, acceptance rates are going down, making it more competitive to attain a degree that is required to maintain a certain quality of life.

Clearly, education is just one way in which you must be on the cutting edge in order to be successful and get noticed. This book devotes an entire chapter to education for this reason, and other chapters offer valuable information to give you an added edge in other areas, such as developing people skills. It is only in this way that you can make yourself professionally desirable in an increasingly competitive world.

Why do we need to develop more successful habits?

Consider the development of successful and effective habits as the gateway to all other successes. One cannot be successful without being organized, prepared, or well-educated. Likewise, success cannot be attained unless you know how to take initiative, negotiate, and network. Generally, success does not come to those who have low self-confidence or a negative attitude. Therefore, developing successful habits is the accomplishment from which all other successes flow.

Finally, we need to develop more successful habits because our happiness depends on it. When we succeed in doing or getting the things we strive for, we feel excellent! When we make connections with people who value our skills and opinions, we feel happy, fulfilled, and motivated.

What do we lose by not honing these habits?

By not adapting the habits of highly successful people, we risk a lot: a comfortable quality of life, time, happiness, meaningful relationships, and the satisfaction of a thriving career or business, just to name a few.

Perhaps the biggest thing we lose is the ability to count on ourselves. If you cannot count on yourself to "close the deal," then who else is going to be able to rely on you to produce results? Once you lose your credibility, it is a long road back to recovery. Neglecting to learn effective habits creates a daily struggle to responsibly fulfill your roles as an employee, partner, parent, and friend. Don't risk losing the relationships that matter most to you by failing to become more successful in all of the areas of life.

It has been said that it takes 30 days to make something a habit. Look through this book. Make it a habit to read a chapter, or at least one principle, every day. Challenge yourself to incorporate a principle into your life, and try to do it for 30 days. You will see that this one habit — it could be a strategy, a way of thinking, or something to eliminate from your life

— will make a difference in how you accomplish things. If it is a truly successful habit and well-suited to your life, after 30 days the action will become an involuntary part of you.

Maximizing the Benefits of This Book

Always keep this book handy. Put it in the glove box of your car. Stick it in the top drawer of your desk at work. Lay it on your nightstand before bed. Keep it in your briefcase or purse while waiting for appointments. Keep it in your gym bag. This book was written to be read over and over again. It will take time to affect change, so the idea is to read it and practice the contents often. Remember that becoming a highly successful person is a long-term goal that will take time, patience, and discipline. You will feel better almost immediately once you start reading this book, though, and find that there are more than 200 pieces of valuable information and great wisdom that will help you reach your goals.

Use the simple principles in this book as you would tools in a toolbox. Refer to them often as you need to. Flip to a certain page when confronted with that situation. For example, if you find yourself with a job offer and are unsure of how to negotiate your salary, flip to the simple principles that deal with negotiating and calculating your worth. Similarly, if you find yourself at a dinner party and unsure of how to strike up conversation with the other guests, flip to the Developing People Skills chapter for suggestions that will help you make the most of your social experiences. Above all, use this book to adopt the habits, tricks, and practices that will allow you to become a more successful person!

Communicating:
The Gateway to Success

Though it is something we do every day, communicating is a surprisingly difficult enterprise for most of us. Communication problems rank among the most common in romantic, professional, and familial relationships. As a result, billions are spent every year on industries geared toward helping people improve their communication skills.

Mastering communication skills is possibly the number one thing you can do to become a more successful person. People who can voice their opinions and ideas, as well as listen to the thoughts of others, are increasingly valued. In fact, according to a recent study conducted by the Katz Business School at the University of Pittsburgh, the ability to communicate well was ranked as the single most important skill employers look for when recruiting managers and other high-level positions.

Being a successful communicator will help you be an effective person in other ways as well. Successful communication results in better relationships and improved social interactions. It can also save you time and reduce stress (think of how many times you and your partner have fought long into the night because he or she didn't understand your point or because you weren't able to adequately express your feelings). Similarly, being able to communicate well cuts down on time you spend having to explain yourself to health professionals, salespeople, and employers or employees. Communicating clearly will also help you interact more efficiently with people you collaborate with on social projects, clubs, or teams.

At the heart of being a good communicator is knowing what it is you want to say. Although that sounds simple enough, this tends to be the biggest obstacle to communicating effectively. Many of us have trouble isolating our thoughts and opinions — but if we are unsure of what we want to say, how are we to express ourselves to others? Make sure to always get in touch with your ideas, feelings, and opinions before you try to communicate them to someone else. Finally, it is important to choose your communication medium wisely. In today's world, there are a multitude of options for relaying messages. Learn which medium is right for your particular message. Although email is quick and convenient, it can be hard to read a person's tone. Phone calls help personalize a discussion but are more time-consuming and need to be planned for. BlackBerries and text messaging should be used minimally and only for very simplistic messages, such as to confirm a meeting time. And of course, face-to-face interactions are always the best way to talk about something important.

No matter what method you use to communicate, the following principles will help you become a clearer, more successful communicator. From them you will develop effective strategies for getting people to hear your ideas, feel at ease conversing with you, and learn surefire ways to avoid miscommunication and conflict.

Principle #1

Actively listen.

It is extremely important to hear what people say to you. Too often, however, we tune out while someone else is speaking. Practice actively listening by being genuinely interested in what is being said to you. Give physical clues that show you are listening, such as nodding your head or maintaining eye contact. Be comfortable with silence — not every thought requires an immediate response. Sometimes the most profound thing you can communicate is through silence and a knowing gaze. Finally, if you are unable to listen actively to what someone is saying, ask to speak to the person at a later time.

Principle #2

Ask questions.

— ✳ —

Asking questions is critical to successfully communicating with others. Too often we let things we don't understand go unexplained because we are afraid to look stupid or ignorant. But a question up-front often saves us from being embarrassed later when it becomes apparent we failed to properly understand what was initially said. Don't be shy about stopping someone immediately when you don't understand what they mean. Say, "Could you explain that a little further?" or "Could you explain that in another way?" Try paraphrasing what has been said by saying, "So what you are saying is ..." Questions are the best way to show that you are interested in what the other person is saying.

Principle #3

Learn to make small talk.

Being conversational helps get the ball rolling and puts people at ease. Though subjects like the weather or traffic may seem superficial, the give and take of small talk is important for developing constructive dialogue before discussions get down to business. Also, knowing how to spark smart, interesting banter during otherwise "dead" spaces of time — such as a wait for a restaurant table, a walk to a car, or an elevator ride — will make you seem well-rounded and smart to clients and coworkers.

Principle #4

Address offensive behavior, not the person.

Successful people know it is important to phrase criticism in an impersonal way. Blaming a person for negative behavior makes them feel defensive and on the spot. You are more likely to get the desired result from them when you do not make your criticism personal. For example, instead of saying, "You interrupted me," try, "I feel disrespected when I am interrupted." Focusing on the behavior alone allows whomever you are speaking with to avoid feeling branded as the type of person who interrupts. Your goal is to change behavior, not to make people feel bad or self-conscious.

PRINCIPLE #5

Control your body language.

———————————— ❈ ————————————

According to the British Broadcasting Company, body language is the single greatest indicator of what we truly wish to communicate. In fact, 55 percent of the meaning of a conversation is delivered through body language — 38 percent is from the tone and inflection of our voice while just 7 percent comes from what we're actually saying! So pay attention to the messages your body sends. Uncross your arms. Sit up straight. Avoid touching your face or fussing with your hair. Occupy fidgety fingers with a pen. Open, confident body language yields open, focused listeners. Avoid creating an unconscious barrier that contradicts your words.

Principle #6

If you don't have anything nice to say, stay quiet.

Highly successful people rarely engage in trash talk or unnecessary criticism. This is mostly because it is never beneficial to become known as the type of person who gossips or as someone who is cruel. Therefore, refrain from saying things that are unnecessarily harsh, hurtful, or gossipy. As author Dorothy Nevil once said, "The real art of conversation is not only to say the right thing at the right place, but to leave unsaid the wrong thing at the tempting moment."

Principle #7

Everyone is wrong sometimes — recognize when it is your time.

Learning to apologize is another critical piece of communicating well. We all make mistakes, hurt others, and speak or act inappropriately at times. When a person comes to you with a complaint, your first instinct may be to argue with their version of the story or to turn the criticism on them. But recognizing the validity of their grievance can go a long way toward rectifying the situation and building healthy communication pathways for the future. Many times, a simple (but genuine) "I'm sorry," or "I didn't realize" is all it takes to restore a relationship.

Principle #8

Don't put words in people's mouths.

---- ✳ ----

Successful people avoid finishing people's sentences for them or assuming they already know what someone has to say. They know that often it is appropriate simply to listen. A pause in conversation is not an invitation to finish a person's thoughts. Give others the thinking room to say what they want to say, how they want to say it. You might find that you never would have thought of the comment someone else ends up making. Furthermore, highly successful people are less likely to push their way forward in a conversation — they usually wait to talk.

Principle #9

Be willing to compromise.

It is important to know when your ideas are not as strong as others'. In these situations, you must be willing to compromise. Being seen as someone who compromises is important for building strong and successful relationships with coworkers, family, and friends. As poet Phyllis McGinley once remarked, "Compromise, if not the spice of life, is its solidity. It is what makes nations great and marriages happy." Finally, being able to compromise usually helps make the best and most-informed decision, which is more important than simply having your opinion win out all the time.

Principle #10

Highlight a positive when you must point out a negative.

Everyone needs to be criticized now and then. But when you focus only on criticism, the person you critique will likely leave the conversation feeling more demoralized than motivated to improve. Therefore, aim to make criticism constructive. Neutralize the discussion by starting off with what the person is doing right. Let that segue into what else you need the person to do correctly. For example, say to your employee, "You have been great at meeting deadlines, but now I need you to improve the quality of your work." Beginning with a compliment lessens the blow of the criticism, which will improve the overall communication.

PRINCIPLE #11

Don't be afraid to make your voice heard.

Speak up! If you think you have a valid idea or comment, make sure it gets out. Even if a conversation has started to shift away from the topic, don't hesitate to raise your voice and say, "Before we move on, there is one last thing I'd like to add to the discussion." People will respect your perseverance and will view you as the type of person who is worth listening to.

Principle #12

Know when to say nothing at all.

---- ※ ----

While sometimes it is important to make your voice heard, it is equally important to know when to keep your mouth shut. Refrain from speaking just to be heard — people will judge you on the quality of what you have to say, not the quantity. As Abraham Lincoln once noted, "It is better to keep one's mouth shut and be thought of as a fool than to open it and resolve all doubt." If you don't have anything useful to contribute to the conversation, or don't really know what you are talking about, it is always better to let someone else have the floor.

Principle #13

Know what you want to say and stick to it.

Staying on topic is perhaps the most critical communication skill to develop. Ask yourself, "What is the purpose of my message?" Boil what you want to say down to a single, clear statement that directly tells the recipient what you want to accomplish. In doing so you remove the potential for misinterpretation and maximize your chances for successful results. To practice staying on topic, create an outline of what you want to say, and check that each thought or subject directly relates to your main idea. If any entry on the outline deviates from your main message, delete it.

Getting Organized

An old saying goes, "To know where you can find something is the chief part of learning." Indeed, organization is at the heart of being a highly effective person and is the foundation from which many other key habits spring. Being well-organized allows a person to be prepared, which in turn improves productivity. Likewise, being organized helps a person feel in control, which heralds self-confidence. Applying the following principles for organization to your own life will help you position yourself for success in a variety of areas.

Why do many of us find ourselves so disorganized today? For one, our world is increasingly complicated. We own more gadgets, tend to have more bills, are in touch with more people, and have more places to go. While the Internet and other high-tech devices have allowed us to take care of certain tasks more efficiently, they have also added more complications to what might otherwise be simple, one-step tasks. The fast-paced, instant gratification of the information age has also cut down on our ability to focus on one task until it is complete. Thus many of us end up feeling like we are in the middle of 80 different incomplete projects, and we can't quite catch a breath to finish any one of them.

Streamlining the business of life is not a skill that comes naturally to many people. Because of this, millions of dollars are spent each year on products and programs that promise to help get people organized. A new trend in the 21st century is to consult "organizational professionals" who offer a personalized regime for particularly disordered individuals. But these overly complicated solutions tend to add to the problem while exploiting those who are most in need of help. In reality, there is no magic trick to becoming organized; all it takes is the will to create good systems and the resolution to stick with them. By integrating the following foundational principles with your busy life, you will achieve the organization enjoyed by highly effective people.

Principle #14

Think big, start small.

— ✳ —

Make a big job or project seem more manageable by breaking it down into bite-sized tasks. Make a list with your ultimate goal at the top. Then outline each step involved in accomplishing the goal. Put a line through each entry as you complete steps. Before you know it, you will have completed the job. By building a clear road map to your goal, you can reduce the overwhelming feeling of "where do I begin?" or "what do I do next?" that often accompanies large projects.

Principle #15

Assign everything its own place and put things away.

Clutter is the single biggest obstacle to organization. Take the time to assign everything in your office or home a place. This way when you go to put something away, you know exactly where it belongs. Maximize cramped spaces by using tiered shelves, filing cabinets, and other organizational containers. Avoid dumping things in corners or piles where they can be easily forgotten about. Establish a logical filing system and use it — knowing where to find an important document will prevent you from tossing papers around your home or office in a panic.

PRINCIPLE #16

Learn to say "no" when you are too busy to take on a new project.

———————————————— ✳ ————————————————

Say "no" when you are asked to take on a new responsibility that in truth you are too busy to accept. Make it clear that your calendar is full and that your other obligations will not permit you to do the high-quality work you demand of yourself. Taking on more than you can handle is a surefire way to become scatterbrained and disorganized and threatens to ruin your reputation for good work. Ask to be considered for future projects and thank the person for having confidence in your ability.

Principle #17

Prioritize daily tasks by making lists, lists, lists!

Managing both your home and work life can be accomplished through prioritizing daily tasks by writing them down in order of importance. Before you leave work for the night, make a list of things you must take care of the following day. Similarly, each morning before you leave the house to go to work, make a list of home-related tasks that need to be done when you get home. Keep these lists written in a small notebook you carry at all times; this way when a task pops into your mind, you can get it down on your list before you forget.

PRINCIPLE #18

Clear your work space to clear your mind.

Lawyer Florynce R. Kennedy told her clients, "Don't agonize; organize." Indeed, taking the time to organize your desk, garage, kitchen, or other work space will save you hours of frustration. Take a few minutes each day to sort mail, file documents, throw away trash, and otherwise clear your desk. Create a system for storing pots and pans, tools, or other supplies so you can find what you're looking for quickly. You'll appreciate the freshness of a clean work space when you next return to it and will find it easier to jump right into work instead of getting derailed by preliminary tasks.

Principle #19

Delegate tasks to others who are capable.

North Dakota Senator Byron Dorgan once made the following humorous remark: "When in charge ponder. When in trouble delegate. When in doubt mumble." Indeed, the mark of a successful person is knowing you cannot do everything by yourself. Instead, delegate responsibility to others whom you trust. Learning to share responsibilities is key to staying organized and preventing "system overload." It is just as important to know when to complete the whole project yourself as it is to know when to pass tasks on to others.

Principle #20

Group like activities together to prevent overlap.

Make a list of errands before you leave the house and take care of them in the same trip. Maximize your time by planning a route for these errands, organizing stores according to their proximity to one another, taking into account traffic and other obstacles. Similarly, clean the house while you are doing laundry. Make photocopies while sending a fax. Download files while you are returning emails. Taking care of activities in groups will prevent second trips and wasted time.

Principle #21

Calendars and dayplanners only work if you use them.

Track all appointments and obligations by keeping your calendar or dayplanner up to date. The minute a new task materializes, write it down! Be sure to block out enough time to work on an assignment, and when recording appointments, remember to factor in travel time. Make time each day to review the week's upcoming events so there are no surprises. Knowing what tasks, meetings, and deadlines are coming down the pipeline will help you approach each week's events with a cool and collected head.

Principle #22

Don't begin a task until you are truly ready to accomplish it.

We tend to start activities in the hopes of accomplishing them but get distracted before they are finished. Maximize your time by only starting a task when you actually have time to finish it. Avoid reading mail twice — open your mail only when you have time to pay the bills or read correspondence. Leave emails marked as unread until you have the time to devote your full attention to them. Never start a project like organizing photos or cleaning out the garage until you are truly ready to finish it.

Principle #23

Have frequently used items accessible at all times.

The average person spends 6 weeks a year looking for misplaced items. To minimize the time you waste looking for items, ask yourself, "What do I use every single day?" Gather those things and put them in easy-to-reach places in appropriate holders or drawers. Having to search for a pen and paper when you are on the phone causes an unnecessary moment of chaos. Likewise, frantically searching for your keys every time you leave the house interrupts your ability to focus on where you need to go. Being organized means having daily items ready to go on a moment's notice.

EDUCATING YOURSELF

Education is critical to being a highly effective person. Those who are knowledgeable about the world are more likely to be successful in professional, social, and personal environments. Those who educate themselves about different cultures, religions, and countries are likely to make better managers to a wide variety of employees. Similarly, those who keep up with the news are likely to make informed business decisions at work. Indeed, keeping yourself educated will go a long way toward making you more successful in all areas of life.

Educating yourself allows you to continuously update your "knowledge bank," or the amount of information you have on any given number of subjects. Having knowledge about many subjects is important because it widens the range of situations and conversations you are able to participate in. This is a skill you need in order to come across as effective and successful. Successful people can relate to both bosses and employees;

people in their industry and people outside of it; athletes and artists; older people and younger people. In fact, the key to relating to such a wide variety of people is finding something to talk about with whomever you're speaking. You never know when that article you read on sport fishing or that seminar you took on basic accounting will help you make an important connection with someone.

Furthermore, people who keep themselves educated are more likely to try new things, which allows them to discover processes that make life more effective and efficient. In particular, people who make computer education part of their lives are more likely to adapt to technological changes that streamline many of life's tasks. For example, if you are proficient on the Internet, you can pay your bills online, order gifts, plan trips, communicate through email, and do research on topics that interest you. You can accomplish each of these tasks in a fraction of the time it would have taken without the Internet. You can even use the Internet to further your formal education. If you want a certificate or degree in a particular discipline, there are many institutions that offer distance learning programs with online classes. These classes can often be completed any time of day, making it possible for the busiest among us to incorporate higher education into our lives. Keeping yourself computer savvy can be difficult in our fast-changing world, but it is probably one of the most important things you can do to keep yourself ahead of the curve.

Educating yourself on a variety of fronts will vastly benefit your professional, social, and personal success. The following principles underscore the importance of making education an ongoing part of your life to make you the most successful and effective person you can be.

Principle #24

Become an avid reader.

To read is to ensure a lifetime of learning. No matter what the topic, reading exposes you to a multitude of ideas, which in turn allows you to participate in a variety of conversations and situations. Both are key to becoming a successful person. You can read fiction or non-fiction — both cultivate success. Reading non-fiction keeps you informed of the world's issues and events; reading fiction stimulates your imagination. So, make sure you read every day. Always have a book or magazine on hand when waiting for an appointment. Join or start a book club. Most of all, make reading enjoyable by reading about subjects that naturally interest you.

PRINCIPLE #25

Improve your vocabulary.

People judge others by the words they use to express themselves. If you use simple words or mispronounce words, people will view you as a simple and uneducated person. On the other hand, if you use overly complex words, people will sense you are trying to sound more intelligent than you are. Therefore, in order to be effective you must build a solid vocabulary. Sign up with an online resource that will email you a word a day, or buy a word-of-the-day calendar. Write down words you don't know and look them up. As Winston Churchill once stated, "A good vocabulary will be of service throughout your life."

Principle #26

Keep up on the latest trends.

Each day, new advancements are made in every industry. The key to being an effective person is not being left in the dust. Scour newspapers, industry magazines, and the Internet to keep up on the latest trends in your industry. Get alerts on your cell phone. Subscribe to industry podcasts and newsletters. Listen to the news. By keeping abreast of the latest advancements, you are likely to become a more competitive expert in your field.

Principle #27

Learn about other cultures.

In our multicultural society, those who are unfamiliar with other cultures are viewed as ignorant. Being comfortable with people different from you is an important skill to build. If you have the resources, traveling is an excellent way to learn about other cultures. Otherwise, check out books or search the Internet on different countries or religions. Try eating in ethnic restaurants. By educating yourself on new people, customs, or beliefs, you expose yourself to fresh ideas and perspectives. This will help you work with a variety of different people and gain a better understanding of audiences you might encounter.

Principle #28

Seek out professional development programs.

Education doesn't have to come in the form of a formal degree. In fact, most job-related training and knowledge comes from the professional realm rather than lessons learned in a classroom. Professional development programs may be offered by your employer or at industry-related events such as conferences. Take advantage of such opportunities whenever you can. You will expose yourself to industry street smarts that will give you a leg up in your field. Taking the initiative to develop your skills through professional development programs will put your career on a fast track to success.

Principle #29

Get a higher degree.

Education pays — literally. The most surefire way to make more money is to get that higher degree. In 2003, the average full-time employee with a high school diploma earned $30,000. The average full-time employee with a 4-year degree earned about $49,000. Those with a master's degree pulled in, on average, more than $60,000. Although the cost of college and professional programs increases every year, the investment in your future is worth it. As humorist Andy McIntyre once quipped, "If you think education is expensive, try ignorance."

PRINCIPLE #30

Learn how to write persuasively.

———————————— ✳ ————————————

Those who can write well are among the most powerful and successful people on the planet. Persuasive writing is an especially important skill for successful people to develop because they often need to convince others to see their point of view. Being able to write persuasively will allow you to draft convincing letters and successfully pitch new ideas in captivating reports. Practice making yourself a better writer by devoting just 15 minutes a day to letting the words flow. Don't worry at first about producing polished works of art. Becoming a better writer is invaluable to developing your creativity, communication, and critical-thinking skills.

Principle #31

Find a mentor.

An old proverb defines a mentor as "someone whose hindsight can become your foresight." Indeed, finding someone who has successfully walked a path you aspire to is an invaluable resource. As you experience challenges, failures, and successes, a mentor will be there to give advice, pick you up, and celebrate. When choosing a mentor, select someone you respect. It is ideal that they share your interests and goals. If you have trouble selecting a mentor, turn to professional connections you already have. Research your alumni directory. See if local organizations can offer you a person in the industry to shadow. Once you find your mentor, let them shape you into a successful and effective person.

Principle #32

Be a mentor.

Sharing your wisdom and knowledge with someone just starting out is an excellent way to reinforce what you already know. Furthermore, acting as a mentor helps to continually develop skills in your area of expertise. Sometimes we get so bogged down in our fields that we lose sight of the bigger picture and purpose. Acting as a mentor, however, can bring fresh perspective by challenging you to articulate ideas you have yet to express. Even if you feel jaded in your field, the enthusiasm you will feel from the person you mentor will be a positive reminder of why you chose your path in the first place.

PRINCIPLE #33

Make your commute your classroom.

— ❈ —

The average American commutes almost an hour a day to get to work. Many of us waste that hour being frustrated with traffic or trying to avoid staring at people packed on our train. Instead of losing an hour of your day, make the commute your classroom. Use your car stereo, walkman, or iPod to listen to audiobooks, podcasts, or interviews with people you admire. In time, your commute will no longer be the stressful event you once dreaded but something you wish lasted a couple minutes longer.

Increasing Productivity

Henry Ford, the father of the Model T car, can also be regarded as the father of productivity. Indeed, Ford invented the assembly line that allowed cars to be assembled sequentially rather than one at a time, which was more time-consuming. Just one year after installing moving assembly lines in his factories, Ford realized an astonishing 90 percent productivity gain in car assembly. He saved so much money and made so many more cars that he was able to double wages, cut the workday from 10 hours to 8, and drastically reduce vehicle prices.

Since then, productivity has gone hand in hand with success, and it is easy to see why. Accomplishing things faster, for less money, and for the same or higher quality allows people and companies to be wildly successful, no matter what they are undertaking. Beyond just business, however, being productive is an important skill that should be integrated in your everyday life if you want to be successful. Indeed, our lives are increasingly busy; on any given day, each of us will likely function as an employee, spouse, parent, son or daughter, friend, business person, and customer. Because of our increased busyness, managing life has become more like managing a business. The more the demands on us increase, the less time we have to be a truly effective person. Being productive and efficient with our time, therefore, is the key to being successful in all aspects of our lives.

Because increasing your personal productivity is not as easy as installing a conveyor belt or a machine, it is important to develop habits that will put you one step ahead of the clock. Use the principles in this chapter to maximize your ability to get things done in a limited amount of time. After adding each one to your life, you will feel as though there are extra hours in your day because you will have learned to make more of your time.

Principle #34

Get it done now.

If a task can be accomplished within 2 minutes, do it now. Waiting to do it later is the mark of laziness. Win out over your inner sloth, and take care of easy things immediately. Return a quick email. Hang up your towel. Pay a recurring bill. Return a fast phone call. By getting the easy stuff out of the way, you buy yourself quality time for more important jobs.

Principle #35

Work in a productive environment.

— ✳ —

Life coach Paul J. Meyer has said, "Productivity is never an accident. It is always the result of a commitment to excellence, intelligent planning, and focused effort." Don't neglect one of the largest factors of your productivity — your environment. Find or create an atmosphere in which you actually want to spend time. Decorate to inspire but not distract. Include furniture that is comfortable but won't encourage a nap. Play music you can work to. Although your power to change where or with whom you work might be limited, a work-friendly environment will improve your mood, lower your stress level, and enhance your ability to focus.

Principle #36

Create reusable templates.

Avoid wasting time reinventing the wheel. For tasks you do over and over again, create templates that can be used repeatedly. For example, instead of writing a list every week for your groceries, create a template checklist that allows you simply to check off the items you need. Print multiple copies and keep them attached to your refrigerator so you can check your needs off as they arise instead of taking inventory before you leave for the store. Create templates for as many commonly used documents as you can think of and use them to make your repetitive chores as efficient as possible.

Principle #37

Identify the hours when your performance is at its peak.

Everyone has different hours or days that bring out their productive side. In fact, a recent survey conducted by CareerWomen.com found that Tuesdays between 10 a.m. and noon is the most productive time of week for U.S. workers. Whether it be a Tuesday morning or not, learn when your peak performance hours occur so you can make the most out of your productive zone. Save your demanding work for the hours when you know you are most alert. This way you will be able to give it the attention and quality that it deserves.

Principle #38

Wake up early.

Waking up early fulfills the wish for more hours in the day. Even those who are not morning people can learn to wake up earlier. Start with half-hour adjustments to your morning routine until your body adapts. Continue to wake up a half-hour earlier every few weeks — your body will barely notice it. Whether you begin your day with coffee or work, waking up at 6 a.m. versus 8 a.m. enables you to accomplish more and with fewer interruptions. Some of the world's most successful people are early risers.

Principle #39

Make sure you eat.

A brain cannot successfully focus without being fed. Too many of us, however, forget to eat amid the hustle and bustle of the daily grind — or grab unhealthy packaged snacks to get us over the hump. Give your brain the nutritional boost it needs by eating healthy meals regularly throughout the day. Studies show that a breakfast rich in protein helps stave off early morning headaches, gives you more energy, and helps you to concentrate. Eating lunch foods that nourish your body (greens, lean protein, whole grains) will give you energy to carry you through your day.

PRINCIPLE #40

Remove yourself from your distractions.

It can be difficult to settle into work when there are fun, interesting distractions in the air. But the mark of a successful person is one who knows how to avoid procrastinating and get down to business. As American writer Mason Cooley observes, "Procrastination makes easy things hard, and hard things harder." Especially when it's crunch time, do yourself a favor and eliminate temptations from your workspace. Work off-line if email distracts you. Don't leave the television on in the background. Turn the ringer off on your phone. Handle those things after you have accomplished the task.

Principle #41

Do what you love and love what you do.

———————— ✳ ————————

People who are passionate about their work produce quality results. Look for professional opportunities to let your hobbies and interests shine. Create a portfolio with these projects to showcase your talents to others. Use it as a record of your accomplishments. When others see your skills and enthusiasm, they will be more likely to seek you out for projects. If you can combine work and play, you'll never want to stop indulging the fun! As the poet David Frost once wrote, "Don't aim for success if you want it; just do what you love and believe in, and success will come naturally."

Principle #42

Take a break when you need one.

When facing multiple deadlines or a seemingly endless list of chores, we often feel compelled to "power through" to get things accomplished. A pause in activity may feel as though you're wasting time or getting off-track, but taking a break when you need to can often be your best time-saving tool. Just a 15-minute walk can refresh you, allowing you to do higher-quality and more efficient work. When you hit a wall or feel yourself struggling, don't be afraid to take a break — you will return to your project truly ready to work on it.

Principle #43

Single-task.

A recent study conducted by Microsoft found that U.S. workers are unproductive for a whopping 35 percent of their workweek. Much of this failure in productivity is due to a tendency to multitask. While multitasking can be helpful in getting simple tasks done, more often than not it divides our attention, making it more difficult and time-consuming to accomplish serious work. Simplify your work by attacking one project at a time. When you give 100 percent of your attention to one job, your role and objective become clear-cut and uncomplicated. People will appreciate the quality and care that reveal themselves in your focused work.

Principle #44

Schedule meetings only when necessary.

❋

According to Scott Snair, an expert on efficiency in the modern workplace, today's managers spend between 25 and 75 percent of their workday in meetings, at least half of which are unproductive. To maximize productivity in your place of business, don't meet just for the sake of meeting. Though the intention of regularly scheduled meetings may be good, countless hours are wasted if the messages could have been delivered just as easily by email or memo. If a meeting is necessary, write up a clear agenda. Hand it out to the participants beforehand, and insist on sticking to it.

Principle #45

Take a nap.

Studies show that a 15-minute power nap does wonders for increasing a person's productivity. It's easy to understand why. Without a nap people find themselves burnt out, roaming the halls, taking long coffee breaks, or staring at the clock until the end of the workday. If you are able to indulge in a quick nap, however, you allow your brain to reboot, which will help you focus, improve your mood, and leave you feeling refreshed to tackle the day's remaining tasks. In time, you'll find that the 15 minutes you took to decompress cost less than the hour wasted trying to stay awake.

Principle #46

Change your focus.

If you are no longer being effective in the task at hand, switch to another one. Though you may feel inclined to finish, it does no good to pound away at something you are mentally over. Help yourself finish important work by knowing when to switch up your focus. If you have been at a computer all day, seek out physical tasks that give the cerebral part of your brain a break. Changing your focus lets you come back to the original task refreshed — making you more likely to complete the genius work you started.

PRINCIPLE #47

Know when a job is complete.

---- ❊ ----

Successful people know when to stop tinkering with work that is complete. Avoid putting yourself in situations where you are never quite done with your project. You can spend 2 days revising a report you've written, but your boss is still likely to make changes. Likewise, you can spend 2 hours cutting fruit into artistic shapes, but people are just going to eat it. While it is admirable to give your projects 110 percent, make sure your efforts are going to worthwhile endeavors. If your tendency to be perfect gets in the way of meeting a deadline, you're in trouble. Learn to recognize when your role in the process is done or when you've prepared enough.

DEVELOPING PEOPLE SKILLS

One of the most ironic aspects of the modern world is that on any given day, we interact with more people than ever before; yet interpersonal skills are increasingly on the decline. Indeed, technological marvels such as email, cell phones, and personal digital assistants allow us to be in touch with up to 4 times the number of people that could be communicated with in simpler times of telephones, letters, and in-person visits. Yet the increase in interaction has actually resulted in a deterioration of people skills. Why is this so?

For one, modern interactions tend to be very superficial. That they may exist entirely via a technological device such as a computer or BlackBerry naturally limits the level of depth and emotion they can convey. While convenient, such devices cut down on the human touch that ordinarily makes up interpersonal communications. Indeed, although the Information Age has proven to be an incredible vehicle for sharing knowledge and communicating efficiently, it hasn't necessarily improved the quality of our communications. In many ways, technology has stripped the emotion from our messages and removed the personality from our communications. Without much opportunity to interact face to face, we get out of practice with the most basic social skills — conversational etiquette, common courtesy, even our physical appearance. The result is a lonelier and more socially awkward society.

Because face-to-face contact is increasingly rare, it is especially important to make interactions count. To this end, you need to reacquaint yourself with interpersonal skills such as etiquette and manners. This does not mean you need to teach yourself what spoon to use in a fancy restaurant or how many days after an event a thank you card must be sent. Rather, improving your people skills can be as simple as becoming in tune with the thoughts and feelings of those around you. As etiquette author Emily Post explains, "Manners are a sensitive awareness of the feelings of others. If you have that awareness, you have good manners, no matter what fork you use."

The people skills addressed in this chapter can help you have successful personal interactions with all types of individuals. The following principles target effective behavioral habits that will help you get along with others, produce the best possible outcomes in your interactions, and develop an awareness of emotions. At the root of effective people skills is an awareness of other people's feelings. Show that you care. Say people's names. Ask people questions. Each of these small gestures goes a long way toward making your interactions with others a successful and enjoyable experience.

Principle #48

Use names and repeat them often.

Whether it is your closest friend or co-worker, the most attention-grabbing word you can use in conversation is a person's name. Instead of saying, "Good morning," try saying, "Good morning, John." Studies show that using a person's name when you speak makes them listen more closely and endears you to them. Even using a person's name in the middle of conversation — "What concerns me about this, John, is that ..." — helps a person see himself as connected to the content of the conversation. In time, you will find that people will take you more seriously and place greater value on what you have to say when you use this technique.

Principle #49

Ask someone, "How are you really?"

Asking, "How are you?" has become another way of simply saying, "I'm acknowledging your presence." With so much to do and so little time, we very rarely ask, "How are you?" and genuinely want to know the answer. Set yourself apart by asking the question and meaning it. Even better is to be more specific — ask about a person's weekend, their family, an upcoming trip, or a problem they have been having. When you give conversations the extra effort, you will find it easier to build successful relationships and connect with others.

Principle #50

Don't let titles dictate your behavior.

———————— ❋ ————————

Although the people you work with are officially called manager, administrative assistant, or IT specialist, beneath these titles are people that are equally worthy of respect. You needn't go out of your way to treat your manager like a celebrity — you don't owe him or her anything other than common courtesy and a job well done. Similarly, those in positions beneath you should be treated with dignity because their job is to support you in yours. How you treat people, regardless of their title, shows the value of your character, and the right people will take note.

Principle #51

Answer your cell phone when you can give the caller your undivided attention.

Cell phones are among civilization's greatest, but rudest, inventions. *Chicago Tribune* columnist Mary Schmich has written, "The cell phone has transformed public places into giant phone-a-thons in which callers exist within narcissistic cocoons of private conversations. .... Cell phones cause not only a breakdown of courtesy, but the atrophy of basic skills." Learn to let your cell phone ring when you are occupied. Remember that cell phones are there for your convenience, not the caller's. If you must take a call, let the caller know that you value what he or she has to say by asking if you may call back as soon as you find a quiet place to chat.

Principle #52

Have difficult conversations in the car.

Sometimes the most difficult part of a conversation is having to face another person. Take the edge off a difficult conversation by bringing up the issue on a long drive. By addressing the problem in an environment where you are both forced to face forward, the focus is taken off having to confront the person and instead turns to confronting the issue. When you can neutralize a discussion in this way, conversation is more civilized and productive solutions are more likely to be found.

Principle #53

Use common courtesy.

A 2002 survey by the Public Agenda Research Group found that 8 in 10 Americans believe that lack of respect and courtesy is a serious national problem. To make a positive impression on others, bring common courtesy back into your life. Say please and thank you. Hold doors for men and women alike. Let drivers into your lane. Your choice to use common courtesy is a choice to be a helpful and courteous person. Those around you will notice and even be inspired by your generosity and cheerful disposition.

Principle #54

Be sympathetic.

When people open up to you, they trust you not to take advantage of their vulnerability. Of course, laughing at them will not gain you any favor but neither will a non-reaction. A lack of emotion can be perceived as cold and distant. Therefore, learn to be sympathetic to someone who opens up to you by genuinely caring. You don't have to start wailing when the other person sheds a tear, but you can let them know you care about their situation. Though this level of intimacy might feel uncomfortable, the situation is less about you and more about the other person.

Principle #55

Reciprocate simple questions.

A common conversational pitfall made by unsuccessful people is to have one-sided conversations. Indeed, many people, when asked what they do or where they live, provide answers to these questions without asking the same of the person with whom they are speaking. When you fail to reciprocate questions, you indicate a lack of interest in the people you spend time with. So, make sure you always get an answer to the same questions that were asked of you.

Principle #56

Include the newcomer.

It is never easy being new to a group. Be sensitive to this difficulty the next time someone new enters your social sphere. Welcome this person. Don't leave it up to him to figure out what you are talking about — have the courtesy to catch him up in conversation. Let him in on an inside joke. Ask what he thinks about the question at hand. Giving the new person room to make a positive first impression establishes a friendly tone and gives a much-needed confidence boost to those who might otherwise be shy. It will also establish you as a social leader that others will look up to.

PRINCIPLE #57

Send thank you notes and business gifts.

————————————— ❊ —————————————

Humorist Will Cuppy once defined etiquette as "behaving yourself a little better than is absolutely essential." Indeed, make your mark by going above and beyond in situations that call for politeness. When you need to thank someone, never leave a voicemail or email. Write a handwritten card on stationary. Thank you cards let people know you value their time and input. Always send such notes after interviews and for other professional kindnesses. For larger thank you's, such as in appreciation of a job referral or freelance work assignment, send gift baskets or gift certificates to tell people you appreciate the extra effort they made on your behalf.

Principle #58

Praise in public, critique in private.

Celebrate a job well done in a meeting where you can give an individual a public pat on the back and use her as a positive example to the team. Make it a habit to do this with all members of the team so as not to play favorites. However, when it comes time to criticize, save it for a private conversation in a closed office. Criticizing people in public not only makes them unduly embarrassed of their weakness but makes you look insensitive and crass.

PRINCIPLE #59

Dress the part.

Though judging someone by their appearance might seem superficial, people do it. Therefore, make sure your successful outside matches your successful inside. Don't let wrinkled pants or an old T-shirt become an excuse for someone to think less of you. Shallow or not, people associate a disheveled look with disorganization and a lack of professionalism. How you dress reflects the pride you take in yourself and your work. So show up dressed in a polished and respectable manner. Though dress codes may vary from casual to business-professional, clean, pressed, and matching clothes are the very least you should manage.

Principle #60

Take care of your hygiene and do it in private.

Successful people always appear well groomed, but they do this behind closed doors. So while it's a great idea to hit the weights at lunch time, don't let your sweaty workout become the reason people avoid you in the afternoons. And leave bodily maintenance, such as fingernail clipping, to the privacy of your own home. If you absolutely must address any bathroom habits, like brushing your teeth, at work, be sure to do them inside the bathroom. Remember, you don't live with your colleagues, you work with them.

Principle #61

Don't hog the spotlight.

Author Lemony Snicket put it best when he said, "If writers wrote as carelessly as some people talk, then adhasdh asdglaseuyt[bn[pasdlgkhasdfasdf." With that sage advice in mind, be careful with your conversations. Take care not to let them become overly one-sided or spiral out of control. Be mindful of giving everyone an equal shot at making their voices heard. If you find yourself saying, "I know I'm going on and on about this," you probably are. It is fine to be enthusiastic about the topic at hand, but keeping your conversations equal and pointed is the best way to appear effective and successful.

Principle #62

Alert others of potentially embarrassing situations.

You wouldn't want to speak to a group of people with spinach unknowingly stuck in your teeth; neither does the person sitting across from you. While it can be difficult to alert someone of an embarrassing situation, they will be grateful to you for it. Whether a person has toilet paper on their shoe, a rip in their pants, or food on their face, take it upon yourself to inform them in as discrete a manner as possible. People will appreciate the discomfort you take on to save them from a large-scale embarrassment.

Planning Ahead

Perhaps the most important habit to develop in your quest to become a more successful and effective person is to learn to plan ahead. Becoming a highly effective person is, at heart, being a prepared one. As Miguel de Cervantes once wrote, "To be prepared is half the victory."

Preparation is an effective way to ensure that you are going to be okay no matter what challenges suddenly arise. Sometimes preparedness is short-term; for example, getting directions ahead of time or knowing gas stations en route are great ways to avoid surprises during a trip. Other times, being prepared applies to more long-term situations. For example, preparing for retirement is one of the most important steps young people can take to secure their future. Despite this, retirement remains a phase of life that few are prepared for. The Bureau of Labor Statistics notes that 36 percent of Americans 56 and older are still working because they did not properly plan ahead for retirement when they were young. If you want to be able to retire, you must be prepared to meet the financial demands of living on a fixed income. Take the time now to investigate projected living costs for when you plan to retire and develop a savings plan. Make a budget and stick to it. This prevents financial surprises and allows you to know exactly where your money is being spent.

Being prepared also includes thinking in advance about the steps you must take to accomplish a project. Instead of seeing activities or events as wholes, break them down into pieces. See them as A to Z and fill in all the letters in between — each of them represents a different phase, situation, or scenario you gloss over if you only look at the big picture. To break things down in order to prepare for them, learn to do research, visualize scenarios, and above all, ask questions. When embarking on new adventures, it is perfectly acceptable to ask, "What do I need to do to prepare?" for the task at hand. Above all, don't be afraid to look like you don't know what you are doing. Pretending to know how to do something is counterproductive, wastes everyone's time, and makes you look foolish — much more foolish than asking a simple question up-front.

Start today to make preparedness a habit in your life. It is a surefire way to become a highly successful person. Becoming a prepared person is less complicated than people think. It does take some work, but if you get into the habit of planning ahead, you will avoid wasting time and making more work for yourself. The following principles will give you clear guidance on how to become prepared for all kinds of personal, professional, and social situations.

Principle #63

Get directions ahead of time.

In the era of Mapquest and other online map services, it has never been easier to get directions to where you are going. Use these services to get wherever you need to go. Of course, online maps cannot tell you about traffic or parking issues, but other sites can. Many local news stations host a TrafficCam feature on their website — check it 15 minutes before you leave to see if the roads you plan to use are particularly snarled. To find out about parking, phone the place you are going. A 2-minute phone call could save you from endless circles around a parking lot.

Principle #64

Plan to arrive 10 minutes early.

Even those of us with the best internal clocks sometimes end up late to events. Often, it is due to circumstances beyond our control: traffic, a detour, a scheduled train that didn't arrive. Build an extra 10 minutes into your trip as leeway in case an unexpected event delays your arrival. If you have a tendency to be late, write down appointments in your planner an hour earlier than they actually occur. Keep phone numbers on hand so you can alert people to your whereabouts. For those who are chronically late, know that your tardiness tells the person you are meeting that they are not important to you.

PRINCIPLE #65

Have the proper equipment.

Never embark on an activity without having the proper equipment. Avoid skimping on tools that are necessary to doing the job or activity at hand. A doctor can listen to your heart without a stethoscope, but it's not the best way to make a proper diagnosis. Similarly, you can play tennis with a 30-year old racket, but your skills will be limited. Finally, don't let an outdated computer turn a 2-minute task into a 20-minute chore. If you need to buy items to help you get a job done, invest in tools that will help you get it done right.

Principle #66

Know your audience.

All the time and effort you put into your project will go wasted if you do not take your audience into account. Before writing something, think: Who will read this? Before presenting on a topic, consider: Who will be listening? Think of what your audience needs to know. Consider the vocabulary they have, and speak or write on that level. Understand if geographical, ethnic, religious, or other cultural factors will come into play. Use what you know of your audience to make your ideas applicable to them. Your message will be received more successfully when you get inside your audience's head.

Principle #67

Do your homework.

Whether you are traveling to another country, purchasing a home, or meeting to pitch a new product, never embark on life's experiences unprepared. If traveling, do research on where you're going ahead of time. When you negotiate a house price, know what other homes in the area have sold for. In professional situations, research evidence to support your ideas and requests. No matter what the endeavor, successful people equip themselves with facts, history, and specific examples. When you behave like an expert, people will take you seriously.

Principle #68

Always have a backup plan.

It is often said, "Never use tomorrow as today's backup plan." Indeed, always make sure you have a safety net in place for whatever you are planning. Consider worst-case scenarios and how you might adapt the situation. Bring additional tools with you that can help should things go awry. Finally, always keep crucial information such as phone numbers, addresses, and schedules with you in the event of an emergency.

Principle #69

Use your network of people.

When we get in a pinch, we feel suddenly overwhelmed with the terrible feeling that we are all alone. Realize you are not. You have a wide network of people — friends, family, coworkers, acquaintances, business associates — that you can reach for in times of trouble. Let's say your car breaks down 30 miles from your house. Before you panic and walk to the nearest hotel, think if you know anyone who might live in the area to pick you up. Chances are you can think of one person to reach out to. In calm moments, review your safety network so you can call it up immediately in times of stress.

PRINCIPLE #70

Revise your work.

It is probably not often that you throw on some clothes and leave your house without looking in the mirror. Let your work have the same chance to be polished before it leaves your desk. Spelling mistakes or poor grammar should not get in the way of scoring a promotion or expertly expressing your ideas to others. There is rarely a good excuse for turning in sloppy work. So, prepare your work the same way you prepare yourself. Your attention to detail could be the difference in being seen as competent or careless.

Principle #71

Back up your alarm clock.

Even if you tend not to sleep through your alarm, it is always a good idea to have a backup. Even the best of us have slept through the alarm and missed a flight or even had the bad luck of enduring a midnight power failure that leaves us sleeping well into the morning. It is always a good idea to have a battery-operated alarm clock in addition to your electronic one. Or, try your cell phone — most have an alarm clock feature. However, if your problem is getting out of bed, place 2 clocks in opposing spots in your room that force you to get up.

PRINCIPLE #72

Use daytime alerts.

Not all of us have the privilege of working with a personal assistant. But these days, "personal assitance" is available to anyone with the most basic technological devices such as a cell phone, computer, or email account. Explore the features on these devices to find alarm and alert functions. Most basic email programs have a calendar you can set to send reminders about appointments and deadlines. Most cell phones have a buzzer feature you can set to alert you of an upcoming meeting or date. Familiarize yourself with these applications and personalize the settings so you never miss another event.

Principle #73

Take two.

It is frustrating to arrive at an important meeting and find out that the only pen you brought in is out of ink. Likewise, it is annoying to get to the coffee shop and find out the price of your usual coffee and muffin has been raised to $4 instead of $3. To prepare for such bumps in your daily routine, always bring a little more than you need. Make sure you keep 2 pens in case one of them should leak or dry up. Always carry a bit more cash than you need. Explore the contents of your purse, backpack, wallet, or briefcase to find other things that you can take 2 of. Make sure you always have a few business cards with you.

Keeping an Open Mind

Having a clear set of beliefs and values is important to being a successful person because it allows you to operate under specific rules you can fall back on in times of stress or trouble. But it is also important not to let those beliefs become a barrier to people or experiences that can make you a smarter and more well-rounded individual. Keeping an open mind, therefore, is another mark of a successful person.

Open-mindedness is perhaps one of the most undervalued qualities of today, and yet the need for it is overwhelming on both large and small scales. Our world is vast — there are more than 6 billion people living in 194 countries — and each one of those people presents a wonderfully diverse banquet of thoughts, cultures, backgrounds, and traditions. As globalization, outsourcing, and intercontinental collaboration become an ever-increasing feature of business, it is more important than ever to be sensitive and open to those different from you.

But blending our ideas has never been easy. By and large, people understand that open-mindedness is a positive value. But when it comes to employing it in our personal lives, we may not like to admit how much we struggle with it. Perhaps it is because we are scared to choose something outside of our comfort zone. Or, maybe we were raised under certain beliefs that are easy to fall back on in a pinch. Sometimes, a drastically foreign alternative simply seems wrong. For some of these things, sticking with your sense of what you think is right is appropriate. After all, developing an open mind is not about upsetting your core belief system. Rather, developing an open mind involves taking the time to willingly examine evidence that contradicts the ideas we prefer. When we weigh the fresh issues and experience new things, we make more informed, and therefore better, decisions.

As an open-minded person, you are more likely to defuse a heated situation, possess stronger leadership skills, neutralize a conflict, and be more successful at networking. In the end, an open-minded person is a thoughtful person. The skills in the following principles will help you open your mind in a variety of situations that can improve your success and effectiveness.

Principle #74

Be humble — assume you have everything to learn.

The successful engineer Charles F. Kettering once said, "Where there is an open mind, there will always be a frontier." Keeping your mind open will allow you to explore vast frontiers you never knew existed. Even if you feel that you have a thorough knowledge about a given topic, treat other people like the expert. Ask questions to get another perspective that you may not have yet considered. Be open to feedback and ask others to help you understand situations in which you might not be comfortable or understand.

PRINCIPLE #75

Allow someone to take your idea and run with it.

———————— ✳ ————————

Though you may have thought of a great idea, that doesn't necessarily mean you are the best person to follow through with it. Accept the fact that some of your ideas are better suited to other people's strengths. Don't be afraid to give someone a good idea and then see what they do with it. Avoid micromanaging someone you have told to run with something — that is a thinly veiled attempt to control your idea. Successful people recognize that sometimes projects are better suited to others' abilities, and they have the confidence to let other people build on their ideas.

Principle #76

Avoid stereotyping people.

Be honest with yourself about your biases and favoritisms. Blatant bigotry about race, sex, religion, class, age, or sexual preference exists, but it severely interferes with the ability to build successful relationships. Remember, we are all individuals with distinct personalities and backgrounds that we don't necessarily wear on our sleeves. Assume nothing about another person other than what they have directly told and shown you about themselves. Do not confuse cultural stereotypes with individuals.

PRINCIPLE #77

Avoid stereotyping yourself.

❋

When we feel uncomfortable, some of us have the tendency to play the part of the sad clown. The only way we know how to connect with others is to put ourselves down. However, there is deprecation that shows modesty and there is deprecation that shows a lack of self-confidence. Although your intentions may be playful, don't prime others' biases by typecasting yourself. Most important, be open to yourself as someone whose abilities are limitless — not as someone with limits.

Principle #78

Practice playing devil's advocate.

— ✳ —

Devil's advocate—the practice of arguing something you don't necessarily believe for the sake of making or exploring a point — is an important exercise that helps to clarify a mindset and rationale different from your own. Playing devil's advocate is a method used in the top law schools in the country because it has consistently been shown to sharpen the minds of those who must present ideas and defend them. By inhabiting another perspective, you develop a deeper understanding of where people are coming from in their arguments. In the end, you might be surprised to find that you agree with a different side.

Principle #79

Lose arguments and still win!

—— ✳ ——

You can't be the expert in every conversation. And this time, you might be wrong. But don't see being wrong as a failure. Instead, view this as an opportunity for you to learn from someone who clearly knows what they're talking about. When you can admit you have lost an argument and turn it into a learning opportunity, you still win because you come away with more knowledge than you had when you entered the arena.

Principle #80

Give second chances.

———————————— ❋ ————————————

Alexander Pope wrote, "To err is human; to forgive, divine." Most cultures and religions teach the need for forgiveness, and yet it is one of humanity's biggest challenges. Much of the difficulty stems from our desire to be right. But the truth is that people make mistakes. Being in the position to forgive holds an enormous amount of power. Giving others the benefit of the doubt says good things about your character. When you open your mind to give others the benefit of the doubt, people will be inclined to respect you.

Principle #81

Learn to apologize.

When someone tells you you've hurt their feelings, listen intently. Fight the urge to become defensive. Keep your mind open to their perspective — how did it feel for them to be treated that way? Don't get bogged down in the details of the event. Instead, take responsibility for your words and actions, be humble, and apologize. A heartfelt apology can go a long way in healing a wounded relationship. Apologizing when appropriate will cast you as a fair and effective person in the minds of others.

Principle #82

Learn to empathize.

— ❋ —

Different from seeing another perspective, empathy asks you to truly try and feel what another person is experiencing. Empathizing goes a long way toward forming a strong bond with someone, whether it be at work, school, or in your personal life. When someone tells you he or she is sad, feel that sadness. Putting yourself in the shoes of others will help you understand why people act differently than you do. It will allow you to anticipate these reactions when dealing with a wide variety of people.

Principle #83

Read something different.

—— ✳ ——

Reading or watching the same newspapers, magazines, or television stations selectively exposes us to the viewpoints only we want to see. If you are a liberal, take a chance and read an article from a conservative news magazine. Read a novel if you tend to stick with non-fiction. Let someone else have the remote at the gym. Click on a link you would not normally explore on the Internet. Broadening your exposure to the multitude of voices out there keeps you from pigeonholing yourself.

Principle #84

Don't let others take advantage of your open-mindedness.

---------------------- ✳ ----------------------

Writer Virginia Hutchinson once said, "An open mind, like an open window, should be screened to keep the bugs out." In other words, while keeping an open mind, be on guard for those who might try to unfairly sway or influence you. It is important not to become a vessel for other people's ideas, customs, or preferences. Make yourself open to such things but ward off those who might use your open mind to try and control you.

PRINCIPLE #85

Be open-minded,
but stick to what you believe.

Poet George Crane once warned, "One can have such an open mind that it is too porous to hold a conviction." Indeed, expose yourself to the vast array of cultures, experiences, and beliefs the planet offers, but know ultimately what is important for you. A successful person knows what they like, what they want, and what is right for their own life. Check in with other ways of thinking and living often so you can be aware of other values and opinions that are out there. But never abandon your beliefs just to fit in with a new crowd.

Principle #86

Try saying "yes"!

✳

All of us face situations for which we are trained to automatically say "no." Perhaps you automatically say "no" to the pollster who calls during dinner; maybe you make it a habit to never accept fliers that are passed out on the street. There are good reasons why we train ourselves to say "no" to many situations. But when saying no becomes too much of a habit, it can cause us to miss out on interesting learning experiences. For one day, say "yes" to things you might ordinarily say "no" to. It is sure to be a memorable day of action and possibility.

Increasing Your
Self-Confidence

It is possible that your self-confidence is the biggest indicator of how successful you will be in life. As the British writer Samuel Johnson once noted, "Self-confidence is the first requisite to great undertakings." Indeed, how good you feel about yourself informs the degree of success you will have when undertaking projects, tasks, and responsibilities. It also determines the way you will be viewed by others. Studies consistently show that people with high self-esteem are more successful, well-liked, and more effective in every aspect of their lives.

People with healthy self-esteem allow themselves to celebrate the small victories in life as well as the large ones. Paying attention to all of your successes is motivating and confidence-building. For example, mapping out your workweek and coming up with a time-management spreadsheet can help you avoid wasting valuable work hours. Celebrating the fact that you have discovered this new way to ease your time-management problem will boost your confidence — and will likely inspire you to do more innovative things.

People with self-confidence also know to expect that, at times, failure will be a part of life's journey. The founder of Honda Motor Company, Soichiro Honda, once said, "Success is 99 percent failure." Indeed, part of learning what works is also learning what doesn't. Instead of beating yourself up for occasional failures, realize they are small steps on the path toward greater success. But so many of us waste time lamenting failure instead of learning the lessons imbedded in each experience. Making room for failure is an indispensable lesson to learn as you become a more successful person.

Finally, it is impossible to be a successful person if you constantly second-guess every action and decision you make. Use the following principles to develop confidence in yourself. Learn to trust your instincts and gut feelings. Believe you are a capable person. Impress others with your self-assuredness. Use the advice and wisdom in the following principles to learn how to use your self-confidence to truly excel and achieve success.

Principle #87

Avoid comparing yourself to others.

While it is tempting to look to others to gauge your performance, your best measuring stick is, in fact, yourself. Focus on recognizing your own strengths, weaknesses, and abilities to realistically judge your own power. The truth of the matter is that someone, somewhere can or will give a better speech or score higher than you. If you fixate on beating others or being beaten, you'll never give yourself a chance to recognize when you have accomplished something truly incredible in your own right. Don't let the brightness of someone else's abilities cast shadows on your own light.

Principle #88

Set the bar where you can reach it.

Studies consistently show that setting goals and reaching them is one of the most significant ways to achieve results, no matter what you are attempting. When you set your goals too high, you set yourself up for failure. Therefore, exceed your expectations of yourself by setting goals that, upon reaching them, will boost your self-confidence. This can be as small as running a mile 10 seconds faster than you did yesterday or as big as selling 2 more houses than you did last year. The important thing is to aim to beat your personal bests.

Principle #89

Turn fear into challenge.

Fear is often a direct result of low self-esteem. But writer Henry S. Haskins thought of fear in the following way: "Panic at the thought of doing a thing is a challenge to do it." Turn your greatest fear on its head by confronting it. If you fear crowded spaces (as do 1 in 5 Americans, according to the National Institute of Mental Health), purposefully seek out a crowd in which to insert yourself. If you fear the dentist (as do 58 percent of Americans), schedule an appointment to have your dentist explain what goes on during a check-up. Confronting your fears will demystify them, allowing them to be conquered.

Principle #90

Know when to be humble.

For some, a lack of self-confidence isn't the issue. Interestingly, a recent study found that compared to previous generations, Generation Y exhibits so much confidence that it is being labeled history's most narcissistic generation. The study also found that being overly confident makes people unable to form relationships of quality and more likely to experience problems with impulse control. Finally, it showed that extreme self-confidence actually stems from low self-esteem. So know when to be humble — it is the mark of true self-confidence.

Principle #91

Use positive self-talk.

Positive self-talk is the internal dialogue you have with yourself. *Saturday Night Live* character Stuart Smalley popularized self-talk with his famous sketch in which he said, "I am good enough, I am smart enough, and gosh darn it, people like me." Though comedy, everyone knows the best humor is rooted in truth. If you spend time each day telling yourself what you should have done, what you could have done better, or what you dislike about yourself, stop right now. These messages will stall your success and prevent your self-confidence from blossoming. Because behavior is driven by your beliefs about yourself, adapting positive self-talk is one of the most important things you can do to improve your success.

PRINCIPLE #92

Accept your past.

Your past defines who you are but it does not confine you to one identity. As the old saying goes, "Today is the first day of the rest of your life." Treat every day as a blank slate, a new opportunity for you to reinvent yourself. While it can be helpful to assess what in your past may have contributed to a lack of self-confidence, it is ultimately more productive to focus on what can be done in the future. Dwelling on the past will make you an expert in your weaknesses — not your strengths.

Principle #93

Surround yourself with positive, loving friends.

When you have friends who keep things upbeat and recognize your strengths, there's no need to doubt yourself and your abilities. Make friends with people who are excited to see you every time you greet each other. Find people who are sad to see you go — and be sure to return the feeling. If you choose to be around people who do nothing but tease you, your insecurities will only become exacerbated. As American philosopher Elbert Hubbard said, "A friend is one who knows you and loves you just the same."

Principle #94

Recognize that in your own time, you can learn it.

Don't feel bad if someone asks you to do something and you don't know how. Instead, treat the event as an opportunity to learn something new. Just because you are not a computer specialist does not mean you couldn't learn to build a website or maintain a blog. Likewise, just because you are not an athlete doesn't mean you can't train for a special hike or marathon. Successful people prove to themselves that they can do new things. You only have something to gain by learning a new skill.

PRINCIPLE #95

Let go of the perfectionism.

It is great to set high standards, but do not become obsessed with them. The saying goes, "No one is perfect ... that's why pencils have erasers." Being human means making mistakes. If nothing is ever good enough, think twice about the attitude you are taking with yourself and others' self-confidence. Recognize good performance when you see it. No one is perfect and if you hang on to perfectionism, you just might become your biggest obstacle in ultimately achieving success.

PRINCIPLE #96

Learn to sell yourself.

———————— ❊ ————————

A recent poll of American businesses found that 76 percent of promotions are given to those who pursue them. That means just 34 percent of all people are promoted without asking. Never assume your boss knows that you want to be promoted. Make your objective clear. Ask what paths a person in your place of business can take to become promoted. Make sure the right people know about your professional accomplishments. Work with your manager to put together a promotion time-table. Successful people seek out their success, they don't wait for it to be handed to them.

Principle #97

Keep a running list of accomplishments.

---— ❋ —---

Successful people know exactly what has made them so successful. They know because they keep track! It is crucial to your self-worth and overall happiness to recognize your accomplishments. Make a list and in bold marker at the top write "Accomplishments." Each time you do something you are proud of write it down. Do not downplay that you received a great review at work or finally cleaned your garage from top to bottom — put it on the list. Hang the list somewhere you will see it several times a day. Nothing will help you feel like a successful person like being aware of and celebrating your accomplishments.

Principle #98

Learn to accept a compliment.

An overwhelming number of us feel embarrassed or sheepish when given a compliment. Think how many times you have responded to a compliment on your outfit by saying something along the lines of, "You must be blind!" or something equally self-deprecating. Resist the urge to deflect compliments. Think of the old German proverb that says, "What flatterers say, try to make true." If people think well of you, go with it! Successful people never argue when other people have high opinions of them.

Principle #99

Play your theme song.

—————————— ✳ ——————————

All of us have experienced that satisfying moment in which you play a song loud, sing along to it, and feel spectacular. Find a song that transports you to a place of inspiration. Play it to feel powerful before an interview, presentation, social event, or competition. Olympic swimmer Michael Phelps is known to prepare for races by listening to Eminem's "Lose Yourself" — in fact, that was what he listened to before winning 6 gold medals at the 2004 Olympics. Learn to use music as a tool to pump yourself up before big events.

Principle #100

Take a solo trip.

———————— ❊ ————————

Whether it's to the movie theater or another country, venturing out by yourself gives you a first-hand lesson in enjoying your own company. See a movie by yourself one week; go to dinner the next. Visit an art opening. Attend a concert. It may seem awkward at first, but eventually you will not only feel comfortable being out by yourself, you'll look forward to it. You will discover your likes and dislikes through trying different activities. You no longer need to worry about missing things that you can't get a partner to attend with you. When you make plans for yourself, you're sure to be in good company.

PRINCIPLE #101

Take care of yourself.

If you don't feel physically good, it will be difficult to achieve success. Even when stretched thin, make sure to practice basic self-care. Spend time outdoors every day for at least 30 minutes. The fresh air and exercise will clear your head and release endorphins, which will give you a natural high. Make healthy choices when you eat. Eating foods that nourish your body (greens, lean protein, whole grains) will give you energy to carry you through your day. Building self-care into your daily routine will boost your confidence and allow you to feel successful in all areas of life.

Public Speaking: Communicating What You've Learned

Comedian Jerry Seinfeld has joked, "Surveys show that the number one fear of Americans is public speaking. Number two is death. That means that at a funeral, the average American would rather be in the casket than doing the eulogy." Why is public speaking so universally feared? Even when people have carefully developed their communication, preparedness, and people skills, it can still be difficult to stand up in front of a table of co-workers or an audience full of people you don't know. Studies show that as many as 85 percent of the population experiences sweaty palms, a racing heart, and an upset stomach before giving a speech. Interestingly, the cause of our anxiety tends not to be the audience we face or the message we deliver — almost always, the fear of public speaking is caused by being afraid to feel afraid.

Public speaking is a skill you must learn to master if you want to be a successful person. A recent study found that 87 percent of a person's earning potential is directly linked to their speaking skills. Clearly, to be financially successful, you will need to learn the trick of the public speaking trade. However, enhancing your public speaking skills will benefit more than your paycheck. Public speaking is about being able to communicate what you've learned. It's about being able to articulate your thoughts, feelings, and ideas and connecting them in ways that will inspire, persuade, inform, demonstrate, or commemorate.

While the messages you craft will come from you, the principles in this chapter will help you prepare to speak publicly. They will help you present your ideas in an effective and confident manner. When you speak effectively you will also be able to get what you want and experience the benefits of exposing yourself to a large network of people all at once. The benefits that come from mastering this skill are immeasurable. The following principles will make you a better public speaker and enhance your standing in professional, social, and personal situations.

Principle #102

Conquer your fear of public speaking.

— ❋ —

It is quite likely that public speaking is one of your top fears; polls, studies, and surveys consistently find that Americans fear public speaking more than death, spiders, bankruptcy, and divorce. But public speaking needn't be the vile fate most of us think it to be. In fact, learning to be a good public speaker can improve your communication skills, make you known to people who might offer you work, and even increase your salary. So conquer your fear of public speaking — you have much to gain.

PRINCIPLE #103

Appoint yourself to speak on topics you are passionate about.

Unless you're a celebrity, people won't likely break down your door to ask you to speak at their events. But if there are topics you are knowledgeable and passionate about, seek out events at which to speak. Start small — perhaps contact your old high school to see if your message fits into a class topic. Investigate local clubs or organizations that will also put you in contact with others in your industry. The important thing is to have a message that you want to get out there. By participating in these events you start to make a name for yourself, expose yourself to potential contacts, and get free advertisement.

Principle #104

Reserve smaller rooms when possible.

Strive to make your presentations as personal as possible. Avoid speaking in a space larger than necessary. Smaller rooms create a more intimate atmosphere, which will heighten the energy and emotion of an audience. Speaking in a smaller space will also allow you to make eye contact with your audience, an important personal touch. If 25 people are expected to attend your presentation, find a space with a maximum capacity of 30 instead of 100. A crowded room will seem more impressive than an empty hall. People will be more inclined to remember a full house rather than an auditorium of empty seats.

Principle #105

Know your audience.

Knowing who will be listening to your presentation is the single most important thing you can do to make it a success. All the time and effort you put into your presentation will be wasted if you do not take your audience into account. Think of what your audience needs to know. Consider the vocabulary they have, and speak at that level. Use what you know of your audience to make your ideas applicable to them. Is their attendance mandatory? Your audience will be more receptive if you take the trouble to learn something about their background and needs.

Principle #106

Practice makes perfect.

It is tempting to assume that Apple CEO Steve Jobs is a natural, casual person. After all, that's the impression he gives with his hip, friendly, and enthusiastic keynote speeches. But he has repeatedly admitted that the comfort and informality he is able to achieve only comes after hours of hard work and practice. Learn to come off as a comfortable speaker by practicing in advance. Time yourself; remember to speak slowly. Practice pronunciation, and review all props and audiovisuals in advance. Train yourself to eliminate the "ums" and "uhs" of your speech. The more you practice, the more successful your delivery.

PRINCIPLE #107

Be prepared to ad-lib.

Leave some wiggle room in your speech for improvisation and audience participation. Anyone can read a speech from a piece of paper — set yourself apart by demonstrating your flexibility, sense of humor, and critical-thinking skills on the spot. Take the time to elaborate on a point (although keep your time limit in mind). Acknowledging a distraction — such as a loud ceiling fan — can provide comic relief and downplay the distraction. Throw questions out to the audience to keep them actively engaged. Show that you are comfortable flying by the seat of your pants — the trick is to prepare ahead of time to seem this way!

Principle #108

Preview your venue.

Don't make your presentation the first time you set foot in your speaking environment. Visit the site of your presentation ahead of time. Get to know the layout, acoustics, and general feel of the space. If you know in advance that the podium is short, you can take measures to either fix the problem or alter your presentation to be podium-free so it's not a distraction to you or the audience. The size of the space will also help determine how big your gestures and how loud your voice should be. Finally, visiting the space will enable you to visualize the site of your future success in advance.

Principle #109

Meet and greet your audience.

No matter the size, arrive early to meet and greet your audience. Introducing yourself personally is a great way to develop a connection with your audience from the beginning. Position yourself and anyone else on your team at the entrance and welcome participants with a warm smile and firm handshake. Members of the audience will appreciate the personalized and friendly tone you set by approaching them individually. They will mirror a friendly tone with you — a great source of comfort for any last-minute jitters you might experience before speaking.

Principle #110

Start strong and end strong.

The goal of starting and ending strong is to make good first and last impressions — it helps sell the audience on why they should listen to you. Avoid generic openers such as, "I'm here to talk to you today about ..." The audience knows what you're there to talk about — otherwise they wouldn't be there to listen to you. Find new and edgy ways to grab their attention. Start them off on the edge of their seats. Likewise, deliver an ending that inspires or leaves them wanting more in order to make your presentation a memorable success.

Principle #111

Keep it simple.

Oftentimes, the pressure of having to remember everything that you want to say is part of what revs up the nerves before speaking publicly. Simplify things for both you and your audience by choosing 3 main points that you wish to convey. Emphasize these points with gestures and repeat them in varying tones of voice. Focus on using clear, simple language to make a message that will be understood by every member of the audience. You would not want an unfamiliar word to distract anyone from listening to one of the most important points of your presentation.

Principle #112

Use audiovisuals.

No matter how groundbreaking your message might be, audience members generally need their attention recaptured every 2 to 4 minutes. Audiovisuals are an excellent tool to keep people interested in your message. Arrive early to ensure that all the equipment you need is there and in working order. Use props, music, sound effects, and other stimuli to get your message across. Hand out samples that appeal to the sense of touch or taste to drive home a particularly important metaphor within your message. Anything you can do to appeal to the senses perks up an audience, resulting in a more successful presentation.

Principle #113

Always have an anecdote ready to personalize the topic.

Anecdotes — personalized stories that make the point of the topic you are covering — are an excellent vehicle for delivering information to others. Research has shown that people listen more intently to anecdotes than to other kinds of information (such as facts, statistics, or studies) because they can personally relate to them. Use anecdotes to really talk to your audience rather than merely lecturing to them. Tell personal stories that underscore your main points. Stories allow both you and the audience to get lost in a moment, making your presentation a true experience. In this way, they will be more likely to remember your message.

Principle #114

Be prepared for Q & A.

It is important to leave time for a question and answer session at the end of your speech. It is the last chance you have to clarify your main points and make a lasting impression. Before your speech, anticipate what questions might be raised afterward. Be aware of what you weren't able to cover in depth — people will likely ask about it. Be prepared to defend your ideas and come equipped with the sources from which you got your information. If you don't know an answer to a question, be honest about it. Promise to get back to the person once you find out more information.

Taking Risks

Artist Charles DuBois once advised his fellow Americans to "be able at any moment to sacrifice what we are for what we could become." Risk-takers such as DuBois are beloved in American culture. Most movies, television shows, books, and folklore feature risk-takers we admire and aspire to be like. This is because most of us are not comfortable taking risks. And for good reason — to take a risk is potentially to fail, lose money, be embarrassed, or become brokenhearted.

When did we become so afraid of trying? Studies show that adolescence is when most people begin to fear taking risks. As children, we are asked to take risks all the time. Every day is a new situation with myriad learning opportunities. We try things, we fall down, we get back up — it is only with time that we learn to avoid falling in the first place.

While it is good to prevent activities or situations you know will bring you harm, it is detrimental to silence the part of you that tries things even when there is potential to fail. Taking risks is one of the most important things we can do as adults — there is no surer way to improve our lives, find love, or make a fortune. All successful people have taken risks to get where they are — risks that have paid off.

It is important to redevelop the part of you that once knew how to take risks. Recapture that spirit by jumping into the unknown and challenging yourself — if the end result is personal growth and a greater confidence in yourself (which it almost always is), there is absolutely nothing to lose. Taking risks rocks the boat, but boats do not get to their destination without leaving shore. The following principles will help you learn the art of taking risks — practice instilling them in your everyday routine to see where the unexpected paths in life can take you.

Principle #115

Lose your inhibitions.

There is a reason why people often have loose lips when they drink too much — their inhibitions are thrown to the wind! In many cases, our inhibitions prevent us from making a fool of ourselves or from saying the wrong thing. In this way, they are a good safety net. In other cases, however, our inhibitions prevent us from trying new things. We preemptively tell ourselves it won't work, or we'll look stupid, or it's too much trouble. So when it feels right, toss your inhibitions out for an hour or two — you are guaranteed to have an out-of-the-ordinary experience.

Principle #116

Take intelligent risks.

The best kind of risk is an intelligent one — one in which you can evaluate what there is to lose. While you cannot be completely sure of an outcome, at times you can make a safe bet that the odds will be in your favor. Calculate your odds by making a list of the potential financial, emotional, and physical losses. If it seems you can afford the loss and still maintain a balanced life in all of these categories, it is probably an intelligent risk to take. Assessing what there is to lose will help you avoid reckless risk-taking that might leave you struggling to meet basic needs.

Principle #117

Go first.

Because we all approach risk with different attitudes and methods, it does you no good to watch someone else take the plunge first. In fact, watching someone else try first can either put you off of trying for yourself or make you wish you had been the brave one. Therefore, make it a habit to be the first to dive right in. Volunteer for the risky project; put yourself at the helm of new initiatives. Even if you fail, you will be remembered as the one who was brave enough to try.

Principle #118

Don't be afraid to fail — you will sometimes.

Former quarterback Jim McMahon put it best when he said, "Yes, risk-taking is inherently failure-prone. Otherwise, it would be called sure-thing-taking." Of course, the entire reason why something is considered a risk is because you cannot predict what will happen. It's true, the outcome might be failure. The upside to failure, however, is that you always learn something in the process. Demystify failure. Realize it is no big deal to mess up, and try again. Once you become unafraid of failure, it won't hold you back from taking risks that are bound to end up successful.

PRINCIPLE #119

Think outside the box.

Successful people rarely follow in the footsteps of others. They make their own tracks! Some of the best risks you can take are the ones where you rethink the rules of the game. Break rules and conventions on a daily basis. You will likely generate enthusiasm by enacting new ideas. Those who prefer the safety and comfort of staying inside the box might discourage you, but don't let them stop you from pursuing an idea you know in your heart is a winner. Those same people will likely come to you in the future for new ideas when they are sick of looking at the same 4 familiar walls.

PRINCIPLE #120

Commit yourself.

※

Putting your toe in the water is not the same as going for a swim. Most failure happens because people do not fully commit themselves to their idea and follow through. When you consider taking a risk, ask yourself if you are prepared to go 100 percent of the way to see the idea to completion. It does not mean that the idea has to take over your life. It just means that if you really want it to succeed, you cannot be tentative or hesitant.

Principle #121

Nothing ventured is truly nothing gained.

We have all heard the phrase nothing ventured, nothing gained, but think for a minute what it means. If you don't try, you won't achieve. If you don't ask, you'll never know. Don't be someone who keeps their ideas, thoughts, and dreams bottled up inside. Remember that successful risk-takers are the ones who act on the ideas that other people don't and ask for things others won't. In that sense, there is very little risk in choosing to follow your heart. As novelist Erica Jong has written, "If you don't risk anything, you risk even more."

PRINCIPLE #122

Recognize that intelligent people take risks.

Though some may call you crazy or even stupid for taking risks, take comfort in knowing that risk-taking is a quality that goes hand in hand with being intelligent. In fact, a 2005 study undertaken at the MIT Sloan School of Management that studied patterns of risk-taking in both men and women found that risk-takers were likely to have higher IQs than non-risk-takers. So don't be afraid to take chances — consider it a sign of your intelligence.

Principle #123

Own your risks.

Successful people never backpedal on their decision to take a chance. They accept the consequences of whatever happens. In other words, they own their risks, and you must learn to do so as well. Accept that sometimes your risks will reward you and other times they won't. Never regret taking a risk after the fact. This type of remorse is the mark of a weak person, not a successful one. Recognize that for better or worse, exploring new territory is a necessary part of being a successful person.

Principle #124

Look ahead — way ahead.

There are some risks that will produce immediate results. Deciding to take the plunge and go skydiving, for example, will give you immediate feedback. But when considering larger financial, business, or personal risks, it is important to ask yourself what difference the risk will make in the course of your lifetime. Allow yourself years, or even a lifetime, to evaluate the success of taking a chance, in addition to what changes in your life over time might improve the likelihood of your success. So think long term when considering certain risks, such as buying a home or starting a business. The success of these endeavors cannot be judged in a short time frame.

Principle #125

Do something new every day.

Go outside your safety zone to expose yourself to new endeavors. For example, if you are a computer person, try a creative writing class; if you have never been athletic, join a gym. Pushing the boundaries of your life can open doors you never knew existed. During any one of these new endeavors, you will likely meet people who will unexpectedly influence you. Live your life as if there is something to be discovered with every decision. You will later be surprised at how seemingly random decisions and risks helped shape your personality. As Robert Louis Stevenson wrote, "The mark of a good action is that it appears inevitable in retrospect."

Principle #126

Wing it.

To take risks, you needn't have every step figured out. In fact, sometimes the best plan is just to figure it out as you go. Successful people don't get bogged down in the details. While they are prepared for certain emergencies, they are also comfortable winging it. When you cruise without a plan, you allow yourself to be more creative and discover ideas you might have skipped had you mapped out your whole route. You might be surprised to see how unplanned, time-pressured opportunities unlock your most creative and innovative sides.

Negotiating

Negotiation is a necessary part of the highly effective and successful person's life. Still, many of us dread it, because we are uncomfortable with confrontation. But it is unrealistic to think you can go through life without negotiating. Therefore, the sooner you learn to be a savvy negotiator, the better.

Learning how to successfully negotiate a deal is necessary to all areas of life. You will need to negotiate a raise at your job (or a starting salary if you are just being hired). You will need to negotiate the price of a home or car you buy or sell. All of these transactions require negotiation skills. In each of these situations, think of negotiating not as a confrontational exchange but as a win-win situation. After all, you and the person with whom you are trying to broker a deal both stand to gain something from the interaction. Of course, it is much easier to drive a hard bargain when you could just as easily walk away from the situation. So to get comfortable with negotiating, practice on something you don't want all that much. Try out your negotiating skills at a swap meet or garage sale. Sure, it might feel petty to haggle over an old lamp, but remember it is going toward a good cause: building your negotiating skills.

Some hard and fast rules for negotiating include always being willing to walk away from a deal if you do not stand to gain from it. Also, never enter a negotiation when you are desperate! You are certain to lose out if the other party senses you are at a disadvantage. Finally, come to the negotiating table armed with information to back up your perspective. These and other strategies are discussed in the following chapter. Follow these principles to learn how to successfully negotiate for what you want.

PRINCIPLE #127

Create a game plan.

Author Richard Shell has defined negotiation as "a kind of universal dance with 4 stages or steps. And it works best when both parties are experienced dancers." According to Shell, the 4 stages critical to negotiating are preparation, information exchange, explicit bargaining, and commitment. Work these stages into whatever you are negotiating. Take care not to skip any of them — each is important for building your case regarding why you should get what you want.

PRINCIPLE #128

Be flexible, but don't be a pushover.

Statistically speaking, a cooperative negotiator is more effective at sealing a deal than a competitive one. Research shows that people who are flexible make better deals than those who are not. Make it clear that you are willing to work toward a mutual solution, but keep your guard up. A solution that involves compromise may not be what you envisioned, and sometimes it may not be to your advantage. If you feel your compromise means you must give up too much, give up the compromise.

Principle #129

It's not all about money.

While salary, price, and compensation are often the center of a negotiation, there are other equally important things that can be brought to the negotiating table. If you get stuck in the money department, try negotiating one of the following to sweeten the deal: vacation, flex-time, office space, commission, managing others, commute time, in-office hours, sick time, assistants, stock options, insurance, equipment, and title. You might find that being satisfied in the following areas will make up for not being able to negotiate your ideal salary.

Principle #130

Aim for a win-win situation.

The trust you create in a win-win situation is perhaps more valuable in the long run than the needs you satisfy now. Therefore, work hard to satisfy both parties when negotiating. Whether the negotiation takes place with your boss, a potential client, a partner, or your child, listen to their needs and acknowledge the value of their perspective. Then, clearly express your own needs and make sure they understand them. Ask, "How can we make this work for both of us?" The other person will appreciate someone who respects their position and will be more likely to make compromises in your favor.

PRINCIPLE #131

Sell the other parties on what's in it for them.

Always frame your negotiations as if the other party has something to gain as well. For example, if you ask your boss for time off to shop for a new car, he or she might raise a suspicious eyebrow. But if you frame the situation as one that has benefits for your employer, you might have more luck. Tell your boss that a new car will get you to work on time and allow you to stay later. It will also cut down on the stress of having to take public transportation, resulting in a happier, more productive employee. Always include what the other party has to gain when you negotiate.

PRINCIPLE #132

Negotiate with your mind, not your heart.

The biggest reason people dislike negotiating is because they are afraid they will be seen as a grubby, selfish person. Successful people realize that negotiating is not a personal endeavor but a business one. It is important to negotiate with your mind and your pocketbook, not your heart. When negotiating, emotions do sometimes run high. In these situations, take a break for a quick walk, grab some water, or take some deep breaths. Keep your mind in check; keep your emotions from pushing you over your boundaries; and avoid making any rash decisions that might ultimately sabotage the negotiation.

Principle #133

Don't let your gender scare you away from the negotiating table.

Though some women are terrific negotiators, many view it as highly unpleasant. When asked to liken the process of negotiating to something, men in one study described negotiating like winning a ball game or a wrestling match, while women likened it to going to the dentist. Because they dislike it so, they negotiate less. Men initiate negotiations about 4 times more often than women, and 20 percent of adult women say they never negotiate at all. So ladies, get out there and negotiate — remember, you are worth every bit as much as men.

PRINCIPLE #134

Separate people from the negotiating process.

The person on the other end of the deal might be your worst enemy or best friend. Either way, negotiation is a question of what, why, how, and when a solution will be decided — it should never be one of who is involved. Learn to shut off the part of you that views the one across the table as being personally significant to you. For the 10 or 20 minutes you negotiate, view them only as the person in the way of you getting what you want.

Principle #135

Don't be afraid to ask for too much.

Be generous to yourself when determining how much you want to be paid. Once you name your price, it will be difficult to negotiate up, and the long-term effects of the final number could be enormous over time. Research the going rate as well as what your skill set is worth. Get a sense of how badly your services are needed. Don't be afraid to shoot high — if you ask for too much, they might talk you down to a price that is still higher than what you would have received had you asked for too little.

Principle #136

Never negotiate from the standpoint of need.

The key to a successful negotiation is to always be able to walk away. But if you are desperate, you lose this critical piece of the negotiating puzzle. Being desperate during a negotiation is no negotiation at all — it is more like being subject to another person's whim. Avoid entering negotiations when you are desperate. You will surely regret it when you come into a position of better standing.

PRINCIPLE #137

Avoid ultimatums.

—— ✳ ——

Ultimatums — threats or unrealistic promises made in the course of a discussion — are a tool for people who are weak negotiators. Ultimatums are similar to childish tantrums, thrown because you did not get what you wanted from someone. Adults must learn how to negotiate without resorting to ultimatums. Nine times out of 10, you will not follow through with your threat anyway, which only reduces your credibility. If you are on the other side of the offer, refuse to deal in terms of ultimatums. Because the person is unwilling to follow basic negotiating protocol, it is probably not worth working with him or her anyway.

Principle #138

Don't back yourself into a corner.

Part of negotiating is learning how to bluff. For example, during the course of a negotiation, you may say you will not accept a job for so little money. This may or may not be true, of course; the idea is to get the employer to raise the figure so as to keep you at the table. However, you must always be prepared for your bluff to be called. Therefore, make sure never to back yourself into a corner you cannot get out of. Nothing will ruin your negotiating credibility faster than being forced to go back on a condition you have set.

Principle #139

Anything can be negotiated.

An old Latin maxim goes, "Everything is worth what its purchaser will pay for." So make an offer! For example, tell your landlord you will mow the lawn if she knocks $40 off your rent. With a little creative thinking, it is easy to find ways to negotiate small-scale wants and needs — and great practice for the bigger ones. Above all, always negotiate your salary. Studies show that by not negotiating a salary, an individual stands to lose more than $500,000 by age 60! Don't miss out on what life has to offer by being afraid to negotiate — all you have to lose is success and opportunity.

The Importance
of Networking

Understanding how to network will put you on the fast track to becoming a more successful and effective person. Why is networking key to getting ahead in life? The following example sheds some light on the issue: According to a major career counseling company, 70 percent of all available jobs go unadvertised. This means when you look in the paper or on Internet job sites, you are only viewing 30 percent of available positions! The remainder of the positions are never posted, because they are filled through word of mouth — otherwise known as networking.

When done right, networking is an effortless and natural part of your daily life. It is simply the process of making yourself, your skills, and your career goals known to the people you interact with every day. This doesn't mean that you should rattle off a list of your qualifications to everyone you meet. It does mean you should find ways to inject tidbits about who you are and what you do when you interact with people. Let friends know you are looking for a new job. Chat with those in line with you at the bank about what they do — perhaps your businesses will intersect. Keep in touch with coworkers after they leave your company so you stay up to date with things going on in the industry. Let family know you're looking for an investment opportunity. Each of these is an example of making your goals known to a wide range of people who could be in the position to help you reach them. It may not be clear in the moment how these relationships will benefit you — and not every one will. But the key is to start a conversation, thereby creating the potential for a relationship to develop.

Taking the time now to establish a network can put you in the position to find the people you need in the future within 1 or 2 phone calls. You may not see immediate results, but remember that networking is an investment in your future. Networking also introduces you to people who possess a different skill set than you, which helps to diversify your associations and open up unexpected opportunities. The following principles will teach you how to develop, maintain, and use a network in order to further your success.

Principle #140

Realize that you already have 50-plus contacts.

Without even realizing it, it is likely that you already know many people who can help you reach your goals. Make a list of your contacts. First, list personal contacts — divide this list into family, friends, and neighbors. List other personal contacts — your dentist, your lawyer, the people you know from social or religious clubs, and others. Then, list professional contacts — people you have worked with, worked through, worked for, or given work to. List customers, clients, consultants, even competitors. Tally up the names of the people in all the different categories. You will likely be surprised at the extent of your network!

PRINCIPLE #141

Network with those who are different from you.

Networking is often about connecting with people who have different skills than you. You may need a graphic designer if you are not artistic; you may need someone to build a website for your business if you don't know how to do it yourself. When networking, seek out people with different skills from yours to maximize the areas in which you can be successful. Create a networking group and limit it to 1 member per industry — this is an excellent way to get people with different skill sets talking to one another.

Principle #142

Network with those who are similar to you.

It is important to spend at least 40 percent of your networking time with people in the same industry as you. These are the people who are in touch with jobs that directly match your experience and skills. These are also the people who can keep you up to date in the latest trends in your industry. Find these people at conferences, seminars, professional organizations, your own place of business, and even your competitors' places of business.

Principle #143

Go for quality, not quantity.

Anthropologists have found that for one person, a genuine social network — one in which you know the members and they know you — is limited to about 150 people. So don't network just to network — make sure your network doesn't exceed 150 individuals. If you find you have more contacts than this, whittle them down to the most important ones. Coming away from an event with 100 business cards in hand means you've actually created more work for yourself, because you now have to hunt through the names of people you didn't get to know that well. Therefore, take the time to get to know 5 quality people well, instead of 20.

Principle #144

Develop your own sound byte.

———————————— ✳ ————————————

An important part of networking is being prepared to do it. You don't want to find yourself in the perfect networking situation and end up delivering a jumbled story about your background. Take the time now to develop an introduction about yourself that lasts 1 to 2 minutes. Think of this as your own personal sound byte. It should concisely tell someone where you've come from and where you want to go. You can use your sound byte at dinner parties, interviews, conferences — wherever there is an occasion to market yourself.

PRINCIPLE #145

Always have your contact info readily accessible.

———————— ✳ ————————

Business cards date back to 17th-century France, and yet their networking power hasn't died. Make it easy for others to get in touch with you by handing out one of your own. But don't stop there — make sure your emails end with a signature line that contains your contact information. Enter your contact information in your cell phone to send it wirelessly. Be sure to include your address, phone number, email, screen name, fax number, etc. If you expect your information to change, make business cards that list just your name and fill in the information at the time of the exchange.

Principle #146

Treat everyone as a possible connection.

Sometimes the best connections happen in the more laid-back atmosphere of your personal life. Everyday errands at the doctor's office, the DMV, or the auto shop provide captive audiences in waiting rooms. Never hold anyone prisoner who isn't interested in chatting, but don't be afraid to strike up a casual conversation with a simple, "What do you do?" And if there ever was a reason to talk to the person sitting next to you on the plane, this is it. Even if he does not meet any of your needs, he might be able to provide insider knowledge on people or companies of interest to you.

Principle #147

Take a bite out of the big cheese.

Intimidation keeps many of us from approaching the CEO at our company or the speaker at a conference we attend. Be the one who crosses the aisle! Even if you are the "little" guy, don't let that stop you from connecting with higher-ups. The first conversation you have in common, after all, is your interest in achieving success. Treat the situation as a friendly conversation — you're not making a sales pitch or interviewing for a new job. First gather information, then exchange contact information. Later on, your efforts could be rewarded if the big cheese connects you with your big break.

Principle #148

Keep in touch.

— ❄ —

There is also no better way to reinforce your name than by sending contacts in your network birthday wishes, holiday cards, thank you notes, or other correspondence. Therefore, make sure to maintain a calendar and personal address book. Computers or online tools make it easy to store data, receive alerts, and sync information with other gadgets when you're on the go. Jog your memory in the notes section of these tools by keeping your contacts' family information and five facts about that person. Your network will appreciate your timely wishes and be inclined to remember you for future needs.

Principle #149

Participate in events related to your goals.

Successful people attend events in their field or area of interest. These events might be conferences, seminars, lectures, book signings, or readings. Attending these types of presentations will educate you on topics related to your goals and surround you with a jackpot of contacts. Once you put up your radar to professional, social, or other events in your area, you won't be able to stop.

PRINCIPLE #150

Occasionally participate in unrelated events.

※

Going to an event unrelated to your specific field or area of interest can yield surprising results. You might get turned on to a subject you didn't know could interest you; you might be able to work this new knowledge into conversations with others. For example, you might discover from an outdoor recreation specialist that you and your colleagues could benefit from a team-building retreat. Similarly, an art exhibit might introduce you to a new shade of red that will make a bolder statement on your website. Participating in unrelated events opens you up to new opportunities and experiences.

Principle #151

Don't burn bridges.

Though an opportunity or connection might not be appropriate for the present, you never know when you may need to use it in the future. Work to keep lines of communication open at all times, thereby increasing your professional opportunities. Even if you have been laid off or treated badly, rein in your emotions and maintain a sense of professionalism. When tensions die down, you want to be able to show your face in public again.

Principle #152

Reward referrals.

Being referred to someone is no small thing. A person you know has given their word to someone else that you are the best they know for the job. That's huge! Show your gratitude to those who have passed your name along by writing a thank you note, taking them out for lunch, or sending a gift card or basket. If appropriate, offer your own services or skill set at a discounted rate to them. Make sure your reward is in direct proportion to the job you received — a small referral should not merit dinner at the Four Seasons, and a large referral should not be acknowledged with simply a thank you.

Principle #153

Never dine alone.

Not everyone has the time to schedule another meeting into their day. But everyone needs to eat. Meals are a great opportunity to share an experience with someone you'd like to get to know better. Be proactive about talking to people of interest and invite them out for a meal to get a better idea of who they are and what they have done. Or if you walk into a sandwich shop alone, make it your goal to meet someone before you finish your meal.

Principle #154

Create your own website or blog.

People will want to do their homework on you. Give them the resources to do so at any hour by creating a website. An effective website or blog should be regularly updated. It should express, in your own voice, your knowledge, skills, goals, and needs. Likewise, it is important to monitor what information already exists about you on the Internet. Employers increasingly do Web searches of people they are considering hiring. Discovering lewd pictures of you partying or a blog that reveals your hatred for your former coworkers would be professionally damaging.

SETTING AND ACHIEVING GOALS

Highly successful people know how important it is to set and achieve goals. There are many advantages to becoming a capable goal-setter. One is defining your purpose. Another is having an outline for directing your time and energy. Still another is preventing yourself from acting aimlessly and without focus. So many of us lose valuable time because we are spinning like a top without direction. Setting goals allows you to stop spinning and pinpoint exactly what you want out of life.

A key factor of successful goal-setting is setting the bar where you can reach it. Studies consistently show that setting goals and reaching them is one of the most significant ways to achieve results, no matter what you are attempting. The way to set sensible, realistic goals is to break larger goals into smaller ones that you can tackle in the immediate future. If your ultimate life goal is to travel the world, put it at the top of the list. Note the steps required to make this trip a reality — saving money, crafting an itinerary, having a plan to put your belongings in storage, perhaps learning a new language. Check off when you accomplish tasks that lead to meeting your larger goal. You might check off when you obtain a passport, map out a route, or establish a travel fund. Setting attainable goals helps to keep you motivated and on track to reach larger goals. Chipping away at the larger goal by tackling its more manageable aspects will eventually put you in the position to make your top goal a reality.

Another reason to set attainable goals is that when you are able to reach smaller goals, you fuel your self-confidence. When you set your goals too high or out of your reach, you set yourself up for failure, which is a blow to your self-confidence. Statistics show that high self-esteem is crucial to success — and that it actually attracts more success. So experience the self-esteem boost that comes from attaining your goals. The following principles will give you clear examples of how to set and achieve both long-term and short-term goals in both your personal and work life.

Principle #155

Write a personal mission statement.

Becoming an effective person means having an idea of who you are and what you intend to do with your life. Writing a mission statement will help pinpoint where you should focus your efforts. Your mission statement should clearly state the things in life that are most important to you, that motivate you to get from one step to the next. Then, it should reflect goals based on these values. Your mission statement should be motivational, easy to understand, and action-oriented. It should appeal to you personally and emotionally.

Principle #156

Visualize your success.

Visualization techniques have been scientifically proven to work. In other words, what you imagine to be true and real can powerfully trickle down into your real life. Use visualization techniques to achieve what you want. For example, write yourself a check for a million dollars and stick it on your bathroom mirror. Look at it every day. This will not only encourage you to seek out lucrative opportunities but will remind you of your worth. This and other visualization techniques can help build a successful outlook.

Principle #157

Be realistic.

Business tycoon Warren Buffett once said, "I don't look to jump over 7-foot bars; I look around for 1-foot bars that I can step over." Buffett was commenting on the importance of being realistic when you set your goals. Instead of resolving to lose 20 pounds this year, start with just a couple. Vow to walk 3 times this week for 20 minutes. Next week challenge yourself to walk 3 days for 22 minutes. Remember that your goals should be something you are willing and able to do. Set goals that you can accomplish this week, then build toward your bigger goal with each passing week.

PRINCIPLE #158

Articulate your short-term goals.

To jump-start your feeling of accomplishment, keep a list of short-term goals. These can be things you can accomplish on a daily or weekly basis. Some can be errands that need to be done, such as getting your oil changed, picking up dry cleaning, or grocery shopping. Others can be activities you've been meaning to do but haven't gotten around to in a while, such as reading a good book, organizing your photos into albums, or cleaning out the garage. Cross items off your list as you do them. This will give you an immediate sense of accomplishment and keep you motivated to work on your larger goals.

Principle #159

Articulate your long-term goals.

———————— ✳ ————————

Consider what your long-term goals are. Do you want to get an advanced degree? Start a business? Have a family? Own a home? Travel to a specific destination? Write your long-term goals down, put them in a highly visible place, and look at them often. Viewing the milestones you have yet to reach will remind you that you do have a purpose, and that it is to fulfill these goals.

Principle #160

Let yourself hope and dream.

As adults, we tend to let our hopes and dreams fall by the wayside. It may even seem childish or irresponsible to spend time daydreaming. But hopes and dreams are the pillars on which we can base attainable goals. Let your mind wander and see where it leads you. Write down when you feel particularly inspired by an idea for the future. According to Utah State University Human Development Specialist Tom Lee, "As youth grow to adulthood, they should develop a sense of purpose about their lives, cultivate dreams and aspirations, then make daily choices which lead to those dreams."

Principle #161

Make accomplishment a daily habit.

---　✳　---

Make time every day to do one small thing that contributes to your long-term goals. If you want to run a marathon some day, start exercising. Walk at first, increasing the distance and intensity until you are running. Running each day is good for your body and mind, but running for a purpose makes it more fulfilling. Every extra mile you run brings you closer to your ultimate goal of running a marathon. All long-term goals can be broken up into smaller activities you can work on from day to day.

Principle #162

Involve others.

————————— ✳ —————————

Whether it's a public declaration, collaboration, or friendly competition, it is important to involve others in the process of setting and achieving goals. When you let others know you have set a goal for yourself, they keep you accountable to it. Many of us are motivated by the sheer thought of not having to tell the hundred people we told we were going to law school, "As it turns out, I'm not going." Never do things just for the sake of having something to share with others, but do use the people in your life as motivation for following through on the goals.

Principle #163

Maintain integrity.

Hard, honest work shows. And so does deceit. If accomplishing a goal means you must use malicious shortcuts, you may as well let it go. You might "accomplish" a lot, but you will also give yourself the reputation of being careless, manipulative, cheap, or dishonest. As legendary college football coach Joe Paterno once noted, "Success without honor is an unseasoned dish; it will satisfy your hunger, but it won't taste good." There is no honorable future for someone who feels compelled to deceive to get where they want to be.

PRINCIPLE #164

Use charity to define your goals.

There are many reasons to give your time and energy to a cause you care about, and one of them is to sharpen your sense of purpose. Studies show that people who devote at least 1 to 2 hours per week to a worthy cause feel an immediate boost in their self-confidence, self-worth, and sense of purpose. People who volunteer for a soup kitchen, for instance, report feeling satisfied when their work results in feeding those who would otherwise go hungry. It is no wonder, then, that helping others is often cited as the single most motivating factor when setting and achieving personal goals.

Principle #165

Renew your goals.

Goals give a sense of purpose. But once we have accomplished a goal, we can feel stonewalled, not knowing where to put our efforts next. Marathon runners widely report experiencing "post-marathon blues," in which they feel depressed because the physical and emotional intensity of training is over. To avoid experiencing a similar depression, renew your goals often. Check in to see if they are still realistic and tied to things you want. Don't be reluctant to change your goals if they no longer reflect your current circumstances. Always have several goals at once, so if you accomplish one you can turn your attention to a new project.

PRINCIPLE #166

Finish what you started.

— ❋ —

Finishing what you started is about self-respect. Close the deal, especially when it comes to personal-growth goals. If you make it a habit to fall just short of finishing, you will never be able to count on yourself to pull through when it really matters — and neither will others. As writer F. W. Nichol puts it, "When you get right down to the root of the meaning of the word 'succeed,' you find that it simply means to follow through." Find your success by following through with everything you start.

Principle #167

Celebrate your achievements.

Although some goals have not yet been accomplished, it is likely you already have many achievements already under your belt. Take note of these. Pore over them and let them sink in. Realize that what you have done up to this point counts and is an important part of your life's direction. Furthermore, realizing what you have already accomplished can feed into brainstorming new goals. For example, perhaps a few years ago you got SCUBA certified. This accomplishment might in turn lead you to realize you'd like to get an advanced certification, teach classes, or even lead SCUBA trips. You never know where your goals may take you!

Taking Initiative to Make Things Happen

Think how many times you have heard, "I've got a great idea for a book," or "That would make the best invention." People spend countless hours dreaming up innovative products, commercials, scripts, and other inventions. But rarely do they take the initiative to make that dream a reality. Indeed, a key thing that separates the most successful and effective people from others is the willingness to take the first step. If you want to produce a desired outcome, meet a need, or achieve your goals, you must go where effective people go: to the ends of the earth to make their dream a reality. In other words, you must learn to take initiative and make things happen.

The main reason why people fail to take initiative is because most dreams, projects, or other ideas appear so big they seem daunting. People do not know where to start. You may have thought about renovating your kitchen but decided against it because it may be too expensive and you don't know anything about construction or plumbing. However, all such a project takes is a little initiative and creativity. Look into free classes or seminars on home improvement. Buy a book on home improvement. With some effort and initiative, you can accomplish projects that at first seem too difficult.

Sometimes people fail to take initiative because of a lack of materials or capital. For example, they may have a great book idea but lack a publisher. In this case, you still have options: shop your book around to different publishers, or research how to self-publish. It is tempting to let big obstacles stand in the way of achieving your goals, but take the initiative to go the extra mile for ways to make it happen before you give up.

The principles in this chapter look at simple ways to take action in your everyday routine. By keeping an eye open for positive change, brainstorming, enabling others, and creating opportunities for yourself, you will establish yourself as a forward thinker as opposed to someone who does what they're told. Success starts with a great idea that satisfies a need no matter how big or small. By actively finding ways to satisfy a need, you enjoy the same independence, results, and rewards that come to successful initiators.

PRINCIPLE #168

Ask for more responsibility.

It seems like an obvious way to take initiative, but few people ask for more responsibility at work. If your manager is not challenging you enough, demonstrate your own managerial skills by asking to tackle a project that needs to be done, or show how you can improve the effectiveness of the team. Studies confirm that taking the initiative at work pays off. A recent poll that asked the nation's leading executives what they believed was the best way for employees to earn a promotion or a raise revealed that 82 percent said asking for more work and responsibility would do the trick.

Principle #169

Attend the optional stuff.

When you hear of a meeting, lecture, or presentation that is optional, jump at the opportunity. Think of it like getting extra credit. Though the meeting may not immediately relate to your job, your attendance shows a clear interest in the company as a whole. When it comes time for your supervisors to consider filling an opening, they are much more likely to consider a candidate who familiarized himself with all aspects of the company.

Principle #170

Don't wait to be told.

Think of the delight a parent experiences when he or she walks in a child's room to find it is already clean. It is the same delight an employer feels when someone has taken the initiative to troubleshoot a problem without having been assigned the task. Too many people adopt a "that's not my job" mentality — use that as your opportunity to pick up slack. As American publisher Elbert Hubbard simply put it, "Initiative is doing the right things without being told."

Principle #171

Don't be afraid to break the mold.

Most people are set in their ways and resistant to change. In fact, a recent UCLA study found that 91 percent of adults who were exposed to new ideas responded negatively to them. But without new ideas and the initiative to see them through, the world would never change. New products and services would not be available. Strive to be part of the 9 percent who finds the breakthroughs by questioning the status quo or sees a new use for old things. The most successful people, after all, did not advance by doing more of the same.

Principle #172

Make your voice heard.

———————— ✳ ————————

The world was never improved by people who kept their ideas to themselves. Speaking up goes hand in hand with taking initiative. Be assertive about making your ideas known to others. If you are uncomfortable explaining yourself on the spot or need more time to develop your thoughts, write an email to your co-workers and ask for their feedback. Your input may not always be embraced, but you will quickly become known to others as an "idea" person, and they will likely come to you in the future when needs arise.

Principle #173

Don't be afraid to invest time in an idea that might not come to fruition.

Just because an idea does not come to fruition does not mean that the investigation was not worthwhile. Make it a habit to explore your ideas fully, without holding back out of worry that they won't pay off. Sometimes all it takes to make something successful is to put your whole self into it. Even if an idea is not actualized, the time you spent on it may be of use down the road for a more successful project.

Principle #174

Log your ideas.

Carry a notepad with you at all times. This way, you can write down your ideas whenever inspiration strikes. If you tend to think up great ideas while on the computer, send yourself an email to remind you of a thought you had and create a folder in your inbox for these ideas. Even if the ideas for improvement seem irrelevant to your life at this point in time, jot them down anyway. When it comes time to brainstorm for future needs and you get stuck, your log of ideas just might save the day.

Principle #175

Combine initiative with hard work.

Russian ballerina Anna Pavlova once said, "Success depends in a very large measure upon individual initiative and exertion, and cannot be achieved except by a dint of hard work." The ballerina knew something about taking initiative and working hard: her adaptations to ballet shoes became the precursor of the modern pointe shoe. With hard work, Pavlova became one of the greatest ballerinas in the history of dance. Use her as a model for finding ways to take initiative and working hard to see your ideas through. You don't have to make as lasting a mark as Pavlova, but your success will be noticed by those who count.

Principle #176

Put on your creative thinking cap.

———————— ❋ ————————

An old proverb states, "We are told never to cross a bridge until we come to it, but this world is owned by men who have 'crossed bridges' in their imagination far ahead of the crowd." Learn to cross bridges in your own mind. Allow yourself time to play out the scenario of "what if?" Get creative — when brainstorming, never let yourself be penned in by what seems impossible at the time. Throw out your ideas without limits, ceilings, or boundaries. This is often how the world's best ideas are captured to be capitalized on.

PRINCIPLE #177

Enlist help.

Do not underestimate the power of numbers. Take initiative on an idea by enlisting others to help you make it a reality. If you want more free parking in your community, create a petition, pass it around, submit it to your local government, and set up a rally or march. Instead of your own yard sale, organize a bigger, multifamily yard sale to attract more potential buyers. By enlisting help, you empower others to take steps they might not have otherwise taken without your lead. You will be viewed by others as a successful leader for your efforts.

Principle #178

Avoid people that kill initiative.

— ✳ —

Nothing kills initiative like negativity. But negative people are all around us. According to a recent survey, 6 in 10 Americans described themselves as "overly negative or pessimistic" about new ideas. It is important to recognize and distance yourself from these people at all costs. Don't let their negativity impact your chances for success. Recognize that negativity is like a sickness — don't catch it. If it is impossible to stop contact altogether, make a conscious choice not to tell such people about your ideas. Wait until you have accomplished your goals. That way they can simply congratulate you rather than trying to talk you out of it.

Having a Successful Attitude

Your attitude is the collection of thoughts you think every day. Together, these thoughts form your opinion about yourself, your environment, and your future. This means that you are in complete control of your attitude! If your thoughts are often negative, then odds are the words you speak, the way you carry yourself, and your general disposition are negative as well. But if you develop a successful attitude, you have done most of the work toward becoming a successful person, since all else flows from your successful perspective.

Successful people train themselves to have a positive and assertive attitude. This involves avoiding negativity at all costs. Negativity slows down the creative processes and prevents you from taking initiative, following through on ideas, and crafting goals. Negativity also causes people to feel hopeless and without control in their own lives. Finally, negativity is contagious — the people around you will feel your negativity and mark you

you as a pessimist rather than successful person. Developing a positive attitude, therefore, is necessary to become successful in all arenas of life. As Thomas Jefferson once said, "Nothing can stop the man with the right mental attitude from achieving his goal; nothing on earth can help the man with the wrong mental attitude."

Studies repeatedly show that a positive attitude is critical to your health and longevity. In fact, a Johns Hopkins University study found that in people 65 years and older, a negative attitude was more dangerous to them than congestive heart failure or smoking 50 packs of cigarettes each year. Adjusting your attitude, therefore, is key, not only to succeeding at work and in relationships, but in life itself! Telling yourself that you are healthy (and believing it) will cause you to want to put only good, nourishing things into your body. Feeding your body nutrients instead of junk will make you want to be active. Being active releases endorphins, which causes a natural high that improves your outlook. People with an optimistic outlook tend to be more successful and efficient in both their work and home lives. Successful, healthy people have a sunny disposition and attitude.

It seems incredible, but all of this success begins with your thoughts. The following principles will help you develop a positive and successful attitude so you may become a more productive and effective individual.

Principle #179

Practice positive thinking.

It is important for both mental and physical health to think positively. In fact, one study conducted by researchers at Yale University found that people with an optimistic outlook lived 7 and a half years longer than those with gloomy outlooks. Instead of thinking, "I will never be promoted," or "I will never pass this test," tell yourself that anything is possible if you are willing to work for it. Vow to make your boss see your hard efforts at work and promise to study dilligently for your next test. Adopting this positive attitude is a surefire way to succeed.

Principle #180

Commit to excellence.

The late NFL football coach Vince Lombardi once said, "The quality of a person's life is in direct proportion to their commitment to excellence, regardless of their chosen field of endeavor." Take Lombardi's cue by cutting weak links out of your life. If something hinders your success, get rid of it. Avoid toxic people. Make your environment conducive to success and efficiency. Resolve to live life to its fullest by committing yourself to nothing less than excellence.

Principle #181

Roll with the punches.

Maybe you received a rejection letter. Maybe your idea didn't take off. Maybe your best friend insulted you. Of course, things do not always go our way, even when we try our best. Don't add to the pain by beating yourself up. A recent study at Duke University showed that practicing self-compassion may be the most important attitude to implement when dealing with negative events. When things go wrong, show yourself a little kindness by acknowledging, "I tried my best," or "This was a valuable learning experience." Maintaining a compassionate attitude in tough times will help you bounce back to tackle your next challenge.

PRINCIPLE #182

Don't be a naysayer.

Your attitude affects your resilience in life and therefore the outcomes of your efforts. It's one thing to have a bad attitude with yourself; it's another to take others down with you. Author Maya Angelou writes, "If you don't like something, change it. If you can't change it, change your attitude. Don't complain." It can take years to establish yourself as an effective person, but it can take one comment of "I don't want to do that" to establish yourself as a whiner.

Principle #183

Smile often — even when you don't feel like it.

Even when you don't mean it, a smile can make you feel better. Smiling releases endorphins, natural pain killers produced by the brain. In addition, put positive thinking behind your smile; a 2005 study by the Wake Forest University Baptist Medical Center found that thinking positively actually helps people overcome pain. In fact, Dr. Tetsuo Koyama, the lead author of the study, said, "Positive expectations produced about a 28 percent decrease in pain ratings — equal to a shot of morphine." So smile — it is a simple way to change the way you feel from the outside in.

PRINCIPLE #184

Make everyone feel important.

Research shows that 80 percent of the messages we hear as children are negative ones. Given that fact, it is not surprising that so many people struggle with self-confidence issues or cynicism. Reverse that process by recognizing greatness when you see it. Treat everyone as though they have a sign around their necks that says, "Give me a much-needed boost." Compliment a stranger. Ask about your colleague's family or for some expert advice. Everyone is important in their own unique way and they deserve to know that. In times when you need support, the same people will be more than willing to prop up your compassionate, generous spirit.

PRINCIPLE #185

Toot your own horn.

— ❋ —

Listing your strengths and achievements doesn't stop at the interview process. You should continuously make your accomplishments, skills, and successes known to those around you. Project a successful attitude in all walks of life by letting others know how good you are at what you do. Without bragging, be up-front about your abilities and accomplishments with those who ask about them. Making your successes known to others will inspire them to see you as a capable, can-do person — and will reinforce your opinion about yourself as well.

Principle #186

Create your own reality.

---- ✳ ----

When people ask you how you are doing, stop saying, "Fine" and start answering, "Great!" The problem with saying you're fine is that you prime yourself to behave as someone who is merely fine. If you want to be great, describe yourself that way! Likewise, if you wish you were having more fun in your life, then start calling more of it fun. The words we choose to communicate our thoughts, feelings, and beliefs have enormous power over the attitude we choose for ourselves. Prime yourself for success by using words to create your own reality.

PRINCIPLE #187

Surround yourself with positive attitudes.

When you decide to make positive changes to your attitude, it can be difficult to stick with it if the people around you aren't supportive. Take time to explain to friends and family that you are working toward maintaining a positive outlook and that you would appreciate encouragement. Most of the people in your life who care about you will easily accommodate, and even encourage, the "new you." Your positive outlook may even rub off on them.

Principle #188

Dare to enjoy life and let it show.

❊

Comedian Mel Brooks has said, "If you're alive you've got to flap your arms and legs, you've got to jump around a lot, for life is the very opposite of death, and therefore you must at very least think noisy and colorfully, or you're not alive." Life is too short to let its little celebrations fall by the wayside. Celebrate yourself and your accomplishments by allowing yourself to be excited when things go right and let the world know about it. Smile. Laugh. Make a toast. Show the world your positive attitude, and they will view you as a success!

Principle #189

Don't doubt yourself.

Doubting the decisions you've made is a waste of time and negatively affects your outlook. Wishy-washy behavior is annoying to the people around you and does nothing to improve your attitude. Champion tennis player and social activist Arthur Ashe once said, "A wise person decides slowly but abides by these decisions." When faced with a decision, gather all the facts, take your time, and make your best decision — but don't look back. Having confidence to make the best decision with the information available is part and parcel of having a successful outlook.

ACHIEVING BALANCE

Mastery of the skills in this book is essential for becoming a more effective person. However, none of these habits can effect a positive change in your life unless you also incorporate balance. The hustle and bustle of today's world challenges each of us to be superheroes, asking that we juggle the numerous roles and responsibilities of being employees, parents, partners, and friends, to name only a few. With so many identities in which we are expected to excel, it is easy to see why many of us feel out of control of our own lives. To meet the daily demands of certain roles, we neglect others until they come back to overwhelm us in full force. A scale that constantly tips from one extreme to another eventually loses its proper calibration.

Effective, successful people are balanced people. Think about it: Who was the last imbalanced person you met whom you considered an effective and successful person? Achieving balance is essential to reducing worry, stress, and pressure from others, and it contributes to your overall level of happiness. Balance indicates a mastery of most of the highly effective habits in this book — organization, preparedness, attitude, setting and achieving goals, and self-confidence. Achieving balance is an ongoing effort. But from time to time, when you experience a moment of peace and can smile to yourself, you have achieved some sense of balance that many people never get to know. It is during such times that you can consider yourself a highly effective person. That's success.

The principles in this chapter are designed to help you honor your priorities and give you the wisdom to know when to let go of others. Achieving balance in your career, family, finances, health, personal life, and spiritual life will require patience. Your scale will always be in flux, but the following tips, suggestions, and pieces of advice will help to keep you within a reasonable range of peace.

Principle #190

Honor plans with your loved ones.

Everyone knows you work hard to take care of your loved ones. But if you work so hard you don't allow yourself to spend quality time with them, it is all for naught. Let the people you love know how much they mean to you by scheduling time to spend with them. Meet your friends once a week for a happy hour. Eat dinner together as a family. Read a book with your child before bedtime. Though it might be difficult to coordinate so many schedules, your efforts will show your loved ones they are a priority and also give you something to look forward to during a tough workweek.

Principle #191

Make appointments with yourself.

With all the roles and responsibilities you are asked to fulfill, it is easy to lose time with yourself in all the chaos. Take time every day to clear your mind. Schedule "appointments" with yourself that allow you some alone time. Fill this time with anything you want — anything except for work! Use the time to run, meditate, do yoga, pray, or read. Treat this "hour of you" with the same priority that you would a business or doctor's appointment. Spending time with yourself is key to avoiding overload and maintaining balance.

Principle #192

Arrive on time.

Woody Allen once quipped, "Eighty percent of success is showing up." Arriving promptly demonstrates your respect for whomever you are meeting. It shows them you value their time as well as your own. Being punctual also allows you to strip yourself of the stress that being late causes. You will never have to rush, backpedal, sacrifice, or scrimp on quality because you are under the gun. Furthermore, when you arrive on time, your appointments take as long as they were supposed to and never run over. This is key for achieving balance when you have a busy schedule to keep.

PRINCIPLE #193

Hire or ask for help when you need it.

— ❊ —

Being the person who can do it all is certainly to be admired, except for one thing: There is no such thing as the person who can do it all! Every one of us needs help now and then. Successful people recognize when they need help and seek it out by either asking for or hiring a helping hand. See who you can enlist to help you during an exceptionally busy time. It may be someone to clean the house, pick up the kids, mow the lawn, or help with some overflow work. Whatever you need, ask for help early on, before things get beyond your control.

Principle #194

Take care of your body and mind.

How you physically and mentally feel directly impacts your success. Don't compromise your ability to effectively participate in all aspects of life by skipping sleep or meals. While you can survive on 2 meals of fast food a day or 4 hours of sleep, you can excel on 3 meals of fresh foods full of vitamins and minerals and 8 hours of sleep. Time spent eating and sleeping is not time lost. Indeed, the time we give ourselves to eat and sleep makes us more productive in the long run and effectively prolongs our lives.

PRINCIPLE #195

When work must come first, keep the communication lines open.

Work frequently takes precedence in life. When it must, be sure to remain in contact with the outside world. Spend just 15 minutes a day returning phone messages. Send quick emails to keep in touch. Keeping the lines of communication open with the people most important to you lets them know you have not forgotten about them and prevents you from having to spend inordinate amounts of time catching up when you resurface.

PRINCIPLE #196

Take it down a notch.

When you rush through meals, conversations, and experiences, you end up rushing through life. Slow down and chew your food. Taste it. Relish it. Enjoy the person you are speaking with — listen to their comments without thinking of what you will say next. Drive the speed limit and let someone into your lane ahead of you. Successful people are rarely rushed — instead they tend to have a catlike patience and grace. Become like them by taking your time to experience the unexpected. As author Douglas Pagels wrote, "Some of the secret joys of living are not found by rushing from point A to point B, but by inventing some imaginary letters along the way."

Principle #197

Don't be a workaholic.

Writer Margaret Fuller once noted, "Men for the sake of getting a living forget to live." If you find yourself devoting inordinate chunks of time to work, ask yourself, what are you getting out of it? Refrain from working more than 9 hours a day, and take at least 1 day a week to do no work at all. Instead of working yourself to the bone, make sure the hours you spend at work are of quality. The world is not likely to fall apart if you do not check your email or return a phone call immediately, so there is no sense in adding such stress to your life.

PRINCIPLE #198

Reassess your wants and goals.

———————— ✳ ————————

Some of us work so hard that we don't make time to asses why we are working at all. Are you paying rent for a 3-bedroom apartment as the sole resident? Do you pay outrageous monthly bills on a car you never drive? There is nothing wrong with wanting nice things, but if you are working long hours to pay for things you don't need, it is time to reassess your goals. Material things might show how hard we have worked but only act as mere patches for the other areas we neglect. Nobody ever wished on their deathbed, "Gee, I wish I had bought more things."

Principle #199

Practice relaxation and stress management.

According to data from the United Nations, Americans work some of the longest hours of workers in any industrialized country. Our demanding schedules naturally lead to us to experience high levels of stress, which is detrimental to both our physical and emotional health. According to the Centers for Disease Control, the leading 6 causes of death in the U.S. — heart disease, cancer, lung ailments, accidents, cirrhosis of the liver, and suicide — are all brought on, at least in part, by stress. Avoid these and other stress-related diseases and disorders by practicing relaxation and stress management.

PRINCIPLE #200

See the big picture and prioritize.

—— ❋ ——

It is often said, "Life is not a dress rehearsal." Step back from time to time and ask yourself how you want to have lived your life by the time it ends. The answer will vary from person to person, and your answer will help to prioritize the people or things that you value most. After affirming what you value, you will have a clearer idea of how to balance the most meaningful things in your life. Articulate your priorities and use them to make decisions that, in the grand scheme of things, you will never regret.

ADDITIONAL INFORMATION AND IDEAS

The following pages contain a few exercises that will help you think big and achieve success. Practicing them will help you develop the habits and secrets of highly successful people.

These exercises will help you overcome obstacles that are preventing you from becoming a success. Make a habit of performing them whenever you are feeling particularly derailed or unfocused. They will also help you get back on track with your professional, personal, and financial goals.

Practice these exercises to articulate your goals, interests, and priorities; to get control over your life; and to develop the strong communication skills required of healthy relationships. Each of these skills must be mastered if you are to think big and achieve success.

The following exercises will help you think big and achieve success:

Get Control Over Your Life
This exercise helps you take stock of the pieces of your life over which you have control.

Write a Mission Statement
You must articulate your priorities, interests, and goals if you want to someday accomplish them.

Make Time for All of Your Selves
This exercise helps you understand your different interests and dreams.

Engage in Relationships that are Mutually Beneficial
This exercise helps you assess whether the relationships in your life are healthy and beneficial.

Listen in Order to Understand

Develop your communication skills in this exercise.

Constantly Update Your Toolbox

This exercise helps you sharpen all of the skills you need to be and stay successful.

Gaining Control Over Your Life

To become a highly successful person, you must take stock of the pieces of your life over which you have control. Knowing what you can control cuts down on wasting time worrying and making efforts toward the things you cannot control. In short, it helps to focus your efforts where you can be most effective.

To take stock of what you can control, make 2 columns on a piece of paper. On the left side write everything in your life that you have control over. On the right list what you cannot control. Note that the list of things that you do have control over is longer than the list of things that you cannot control. Once you have an accurate picture of where to exert your influence, you will find that your efforts will become much more effective than if you waste time on that which you cannot control. Use the examples on the following page.

Control

- Attitude
- Health
- Weight
- Education
- Who I have in my life
- Thoughts
- Preparedness
- Goals
- Ideas
- Expression
- Time management
- Acceptance of how others treat me
- Organization
- How I regard myself
- Level of productivity
- Risk-taking
- Balancing work and home life
- Nurturing my relationships
- Emotional health
- Financial security
- Decision making
- Housekeeping

No Control

- Other people's attitudes
- The reactions of others
- Who is in my family
- Height
- Race
- Ethnicity
- Weather
- Physical disability

Writing a Mission Statement

Becoming a successful person means having an idea of who you are and what you intend to do with your life. Writing a mission statement will help pinpoint where you should focus your efforts. Your mission statement should clearly articulate your goals. Make it general enough to apply to all facets of your life. It should be motivational, and it should appeal to you personally and emotionally. What you write ought to be easy to understand and be action-oriented. The goals listed in your mission statement need to be attainable and realistic. They can range in scale from long-term, big-life goals to smaller day-to-day values. But in order for this exercise to be effective, your mission statement must be grounded in reality. The following are good examples of things that might appear in your mission statement:

1. I will educate myself every day either through taking classes, reading books, or through travel. I will learn from all of my experiences so I can be as intelligent and insightful as possible.

2. I will work hard to treat everyone with respect and kindness. I will avoid taking my frustration out on others and will focus on positive thinking.

3. I will continue to challenge myself by taking on new responsibilities at work. I will propose new projects and come up with a plan of action for them.

4. I will invest time, money, and energy into becoming a homeowner. I will research the home-buying process, look for real estate in my area, and save for a down payment.

Making Time for Your Many Selves

Make time for all of the roles you play in your life — this is necessary to avoid meltdowns and frustration. These setbacks will stall your work and emotional progress and impede your goal of developing highly effective habits. After all, none of us is just one self. We have many personas for each of the different roles we must take on in our lives. Your work self is likely focused and competitive, while your family self is nurturing and warm. The self you become while coaching your son's Little League game is tough and encouraging, while the self you exhibit with your 4-year-old daughter is playful and silly. Make room for all of these roles and let none of them dominate the others. Encouraging all of your selves will help to make your whole self less frazzled and more productive. When you are more productive you will also be more effective.

Engaging in Mutually Beneficial Relationships

Engaging in relationships that are mutually beneficial is an often-overlooked aspect of developing successful habits. Trying to change other people into who you want them to be is not an effective use of your time. If you find that you are consistently exerting more energy on people than they invest in themselves, it's time to evaluate the importance of those relationships.

For this exercise, make a list of the people in your life and note whether the relationship is balanced. Be assured that time spent on nurturing balanced relationships is an effective habit to get into. Connections that are not balanced should be put into perspective and context and minimal energy should be exerted.

Listening in Order to Understand

Communication is the most important tool that humans have for connecting with one another. Therefore, perhaps the most effective habit you can develop is your listening skills. Listening to understand is different from simply repeating back what you heard the other person say. Avoid imposing your own experiences onto what you are hearing. Practice listening to understand with a close friend or partner. Smoothing out communication waves will make life a lot simpler and more efficient.

Practice working the following questions into conversations to make them more efficient:

Questions to ask yourself while communicating:

- What is the purpose of my message?
- What is my body language saying right now?
- Am I wrong?
- How else can I explain this?

Questions to ask someone you are communicating with:

- Can you repeat that?
- Can you explain that in a different way?
- Am I clear in thinking you want me to do x, y, and z?
- I am not familiar with that; can you tell me what it is?

Updating Your Toolbox

To become a highly successful person, you must constantly update your toolbox. Your toolbox includes your coping skills, communication skills, education, goals, relationship skills, and physical health. You never stop growing, as time never stands still. It is completely ineffective to allow yourself to get stuck. Accept that living is growing and changing to avoid stalling.

To take stock of what is already in your toolbox, write down the skill sets you currently have. These should fall under the topics mentioned above — communication, education, goals, relationships, and physical health. Next to each, write how you wish to improve on the skills you already have. Then, work at adding those qualities to your toolbox.

Conclusion

By definition, a habit is an acquired behavior pattern regularly followed until it has become almost involuntary. This book has helped you break ineffective habits and shown you how to replace them with new habits that are formulas for success.

By now, you should feel good about your prospects for becoming a more effective and successful person. *Simple Principles™ to Think Big and Achieve Success* has helped you take charge of your life, enabling you to be a more effective, and therefore successful, person. If you have followed the hints, tips, tricks, ideas, suggestions, and other principles contained in this book, you are likely closer than ever to achieving your goal of becoming a better communicator and a more organized and effective businessperson. Once you have gone through this book from beginning to end, you should have a good idea of how to apply highly effective habits to your own life. The 200 principles included in this book have shown you that change is possible and that becoming a highly effective person is within your reach.

Reading this book is only the first step in that journey, however. Part of developing effective habits is knowing where to look for solutions, guidance, and advice when you are faced with a challenge. Therefore, think of this book as your constant companion for becoming a more effective person. Practice what you have learned in this book often. Keep it with you for easy reference. Consult it when you seek a specific solution. Refer to it when you need a reminder or want to be inspired. Think of the principles and exercises in *Simple Principles™ to Think Big and Achieve Success* as roadmaps — they show you how to get from where you are now to where you want to be. In order to get there, you must do the work. The key thing to remember is that developing highly effective habits is completely within your grasp if you follow all of the suggestions made in this book.

Tell Us Your Story

Simple Principles™ to Think Big and Achieve Success has changed the lives of countless people, helping them learn, grow, and meet goals better than they ever imagined. Now we want to hear your story about how this book has helped you succeed and improved your life.

Tell us ...
- Why did you purchase this book?
- Which areas of your life did you want to improve?
- How did this book help you improve in those areas?
- How did this book change your life?
- Which principles did you like the most?
- What did you like most about this book?
- Would you recommend this book to others?

Email us your response at info@wspublishinggroup.com or write to us at:

WS Publishing Group
7290 Navajo Road, Suite 207
San Diego, CA 92119

Please include your name and an email address and/or phone number where you can be reached.

Please let us know if WS Publishing may or may not use your story and/or name in future book titles, and if you would be interested in participating in radio or TV interviews.

Great Titles in the
SIMPLE PRINCIPLES™ SERIES

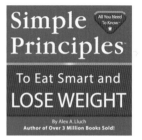

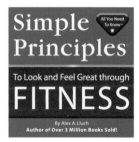

LOG ON TO **WSPublishingGroup.com** TO CHECK FOR
RELEASE DATES ON THESE AND FUTURE TITLES.

More Great Titles in the
SIMPLE PRINCIPLES™ SERIES

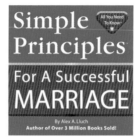

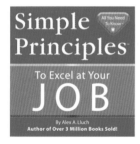

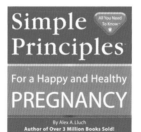

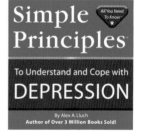

LOG ON TO **WSPublishingGroup.com** TO CHECK FOR
RELEASE DATES ON THESE AND FUTURE TITLES.

Other Best-Selling Books
by Alex A. Lluch

HOME & FINANCE
- The Very Best Home Improvement Guide & Document Organizer
- The Very Best Home Buying Guide & Document Organizer
- The Very Best Home Selling Guide & Document Organizer
- The Very Best Budget & Finance Guide with Document Organizer
- The Ultimate Home Journal & Organizer
- The Ultimate Home Buying Guide & Organizer

BABY JOURNALS & PARENTING
- The Complete Baby Journal Organizer & Keepsake
- Keepsake of Love Baby Journal
- Snuggle Bears Baby Journal Keepsake & Organizer
- Humble Bumbles Baby Journal
- Simple Principles to Raise a Successful Child

CHILDREN'S BOOKS
- I Like to Learn: Alphabet, Numbers, Colors & Opposites
- Alexander, It's Time for Bed!
- Do I Look Good in Color?
- Zoo Clues Animal Alphabet
- Animal Alphabet: Slide & Seek the ABC's
- Counting Chameleon
- Big Bugs, Small Bugs

LOG ON TO **WSPublishingGroup.com** TO CHECK FOR RELEASE DATES ON THESE AND FUTURE TITLES.

More Best-Selling Books
by Alex A. Lluch

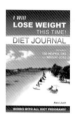

COOKING, FITNESS & DIET
- The Very Best Cooking Guide & Recipe Organizer
- Easy Cooking Guide & Recipe Organizer
- Get Fit Now! Workout Journal
- Lose Weight Now! Diet Journal & Organizer
- I Will Lose Weight This Time! Diet Journal
- The Ultimate Pocket Diet Journal

WEDDING PLANNING
- The Ultimate Wedding Planning Kit
- The Complete Wedding Planner & Organizer
- Easy Wedding Planner, Organizer & Keepsake
- Easy Wedding Planning Plus
- Easy Wedding Planning
- The Ultimate Wedding Workbook & Organizer
- The Ultimate Wedding Planner & Organizer
- Making Your Wedding Beautiful, Memorable & Unique
- Planning the Most Memorable Wedding on Any Budget
- My Wedding Journal, Organizer & Keepsake
- The Ultimate Wedding Planning Guide
- The Ultimate Guide to Wedding Music
- Wedding Party Responsibility Cards

LOG ON TO **WSPublishingGroup.com** TO CHECK FOR RELEASE DATES ON THESE AND FUTURE TITLES.

About the Author and Creator of the
SIMPLE PRINCIPLES™ SERIES

Alex A. Lluch is a seasoned entrepreneur with outstanding life achievements. He grew up very poor and lost his father at age 15. But through hard work and dedication, he has become one of the most successful authors and businessmen of our time. He is now using his life experience to write the simple principles™ series to help people improve their lives.

The following are a few of Alex's achievements:

- Author of over 3 million books sold in a wide range of categories: health, fitness, diet, home, finance, weddings, children, and babies
- President of WS Publishing Group, a successful publishing company
- President of WeddingSolutions.com, one of the world's most popular wedding planning websites
- President of UltimateGiftRegistry.com, an extensive website that allows users to register for gifts for all occasions
- President of a highly successful toy and candy company
- Has worked extensively in China, Hong Kong, Spain, Israel and Mexico
- Designed complex communication systems for Fortune 500 companies
- Black belt in Karate and Judo, winning many national tournaments
- Owns real estate in California, Colorado, Georgia and Montana
- B.S. in Electronics Engineering and an M.S. in Computer Science

Alex Lluch lives in San Diego, California with his wife of 16 years and their three wonderful children.

About the Co-Author

Dr. Helen Eckmann is a renowned expert in leadership, marketing, management and education. She has vast experience teaching in these fields as well as working with both small companies and Fortune 500 corporations. She is now sharing her insight and expertise in the 200 principles contained in this book.

The following are a few of Helen's achievements:

- Doctorate in Education and Leadership Science
- Masters in Organizational Leadership and bachelors in Management
- Consults Fortune 500 companies on leadership development
- Travels as a popular motivational speaker and mentor
- Designs and implements corporate supply chain management programs
- Serves as an Organizational Behavior Consultant to various industries
- Teaches graduate courses in business at the University of San Diego
- Has taught leadership, marketing, strategic planning, innovations and ethics to over 1,500 M.B.A. students
- Has been personnel director for several companies
- Serves on the board of directors of multiple organizations
- Founded and serves on the board of several non-profit organizations
- Provides spiritual direction to hundreds of women as a church pastor

Dr. Helen Eckmann lives with her husband in Del Mar, California. They have raised four successful children.